MIDLOTHIAN
PUBLIC LIBRARY
THE ESSENTIAL
FIGURE SKATER

EHN,

Designed by Compset, Inc.

Printed in Canada

10 9 8 7 6 5 4 3 2 1

The Library of Congress Cataloging-in-Publication Data is available on file.

Ice skating involves physical exertion. As with any exercise program, before beginning, please check with your physician. Should you have special health needs or concerns, again, please check with your specialist before embarking on your figure-skating career.

Nikki and Bernie dedicate their words to the loving memory of Gene Schallehn.

Patti would like to dedicate this book with love to: Mark, for tolerating my obsession with skating and loving me anyway; my dad whose love, guidance and support I cherish more and more with each passing year;and my mom, Dr. C. Mildred Tashman. Every day of my life, your shining example inspires me to strive for excellence. You are and will always be the light that guides me.

CONTENTS

ACKNOWLEDGMENTS

We'd like to thank Karla Schallehn for her precise poses and exquisite modeling; Alta Schallehn, czarina of skating moms, for her innumerable transports to and from the rink; the USFSA and the ISI; Mike Braet of Progressive Health & Fitness; and, last but not least, our editor Becky Koh for her expertise in helping us with the critical and sometimes painful job of deciding what to cut and what to keep.

INTRODUCTION

You know that part in the movie Titanic *where Leonardo DiCaprio stands at the front of the ship and shouts, "I'm the king of the world"? Well that's how I feel when I'm gliding on ice.*

—Jeremy, age 13
ISI Freestyle 5

I work in sales and after a long day dealing with the public I go to the rink to relax. Although there are other skaters present, it's just me and the ice. After a while, I get into a rhythm, a flow, and the rest of the day just fades away.

—Mary Ann, age 40
ISI Freestyle 2

When I skate it feels like I'm flying.

—Katie, age 7
USFSA Basic 1

Combining elements of athletics and art, figure skating is by far one of the most beautiful and enjoyable recreational pastimes. Extensive network coverage of skating events, sold-out live shows, and the celebrity status of figure skating superstars all attest to the fact that this "Queen of Sports" has captured our hearts.

Now you can be more than a mere spectator. If you have the desire, the motivation, the conviction, (and a little cash for your equipment and fees), you too can learn to fly without wings!

Over the years figure skating has brought much enjoyment, happiness, and fulfillment into our lives. But we still remember what it felt like when we first began. It was as if we'd entered an underground subculture where we lacked critical information necessary in order to move forward. Phone numbers for skating coaches, equipment, and "the only guy in town who can really sharpen skates" were scribbled on the backs of envelopes and hastily handed to us by those who had more time and experience in the sport. Unfortunately, some of our first guides in the land of figure skating gave us advice that was sketchy at best, erroneous at worst.

Because we know firsthand how confusing and, at times, intimidating entering the world of figure skating can be, we wrote this book. We want to take you from ground zero to whatever heights you desire in this activity of sharpened steel and frozen water. And we'll do so step-by-step, systematically, slowly.

We bring a unique three-pronged approach to your training. The first of us, Patti, is a seasoned figure skating coach with more than 22 years of experience in the field. The second, Nikki, is a young skater with a significant competition and testing history. And the third, Bernie, is a mental training coach who has helped hundreds of skaters with the cognitive, emotional, and behavioral aspects of their sport.

What we ask of you is patience. Rome wasn't built in a day, and neither were the skating skills of an Olympic figure skater. Be patient, practice, and you will achieve your desired outcomes.

We look forward to working with you!

—Patti Tashman, Nikki Schallehn, and Bernie Schallehn

CHAPTER 1

GETTING STARTED

"But how do I start for the Emerald City?" asked Dorothy.
"It's always best to start at the beginning," replied Glinda, the
Good Witch of the North.

—*The Wizard of Oz*, L. Frank Baum

Figure skating is for everyone—all shapes, all sizes, all ages. Desire and a willingness to learn will always take priority over physical dimensions and your particular season in life. Unless you plan on being one of the principals with the Ice Capades, you don't have to be as skinny as a Popsicle stick. And we have seen children as young as 3 and adults as old as 80 enjoying themselves out on the ice.

The key word here is *enjoyment*. Especially with children, learning to skate must occur in an atmosphere of playfulness and excitement. Regarding readiness, a child should be able to walk in skates before actually stepping onto an ice surface. Once on the ice the youngster should feel comfortable before separating from parent or pro, and respond with willingness when presented with new skills. Above all else, a young child's initial experiences with figure skating should be wrapped in a soft blanket of positivity.

Although safety should be a concern at any age, adult beginners may find that fear prohibits them from ever stepping onto the ice. As you make your way through this book, we hope to allay much of that fear by discussing protective gear, safety precautions, relaxation techniques, and the proper way of falling.

Yes, falling. Falling is as much a part of skating as jumping, spinning, or simply gliding from one end of the rink to the other. Everyone falls, even professional skaters.

EQUIPMENT

Renting and Fitting Skates

The first challenge you will face as a figure skater is the procurement of proper equipment. Many ice rinks offer rental skates at a nominal fee. This is a viable option, especially if you (or your child) have yet to form a strong opinion about commitment to this sport. Also, if your cash flow is a little tight, rentals can be a less expensive option (at least temporarily).

Should you choose to begin with rentals, you will probably encounter three types at your local rink: leather boots, molded plastic

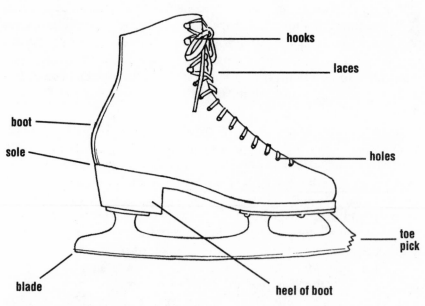

Anatomy of a figure skate

boots, and—rarely, and least desirable—thin vinyl boots. Whether leather or molded plastic, the boots should fit snugly around your entire foot and offer firm support through your ankle region. When you're renting, you should generally request a boot that's the same size as your normal street shoes.

Because many facilities perform maintenance on their rentals only sporadically, check your skates' blades for sharpness when you first receive them. You should be able to feel a slight "hollow" between the edges of each blade, as opposed to the bottom feeling completely flat. Run your finger lightly down the entire length of the blade to make sure the metal is relatively free of nicks and gouges. Lastly, scrape your thumb across the left and right edges. You should feel a slight resistance, a roughness, a slight tugging at your skin.

Should your blades not meet these criteria, ask the skate rental clerk to sharpen them. If an additional fee is requested, pay it. The sharper the blade, the better it will grip the ice, allowing you to maintain control and thereby making learning easier. The last thing you want is to be slipping and sliding across the ice on a pair of blades that are as dull as butter knives.

Once the boot is fully on your foot, pull the tongue up and tuck it in as much as possible on both sides of your foot. The bottom laces (those closest to your toes) should be pulled taut to keep the boot molded to your foot. When you reach the hooks (heading toward the top of the boot), relax the lacing a bit so your ankle has room to flex and proper blood flow can continue into your foot. Once tied, you should be able to slide your index finger between your shin and the boot's tongue. You should also be able to wiggle your toes, but your heel should feel firmly planted in the back of the boot. If the boot feels too big or too small, request the next smaller or the next larger size. (Sometimes, with the cheaper rental skates, the sizes do not correspond with the feel and fit of your street shoes.) If the boots are new, you can loosen the lacing through the hooks for comfort.

In our experience *thin* socks or nylons are the best foot covering inside your boots. Thick socks reduce circulation (which will make your feet cold!) and may bunch up inside your boot.

Buying Skates

If you become more serious about skating and find yourself doing it more than just a few times a month, it may be time to invest in your own skates. Some boot manufacturers offer a beginning-level or entry-model boot with an acceptable skating blade already mounted. Ultimately, if you progress in the sport, you'll want to upgrade your equipment to purchase *separate* boots and blades. (Mid- to high-end boots offer more padding and a stiffness that increases support and stability; better- to best-quality blades increase jumping and spinning ability, maximize power pushing, and hold a sharp edge longer.)

The following manufacturers consistently produce high-quality, well-constructed boots:

- Reidell, (612) 388-8251, www.reidellshoes.com
- Don Jackson, (519) 888-6500
- SP-Teri, (650) 871-1715
- Harlick, (650) 593-2093, www.harlick.com

You can look for your boots in any of several sources:

- An authorized boot dealer
- Internet or mail order
- A local skating club's "next-to-new" sale
- Bulletin boards at local rinks
- A sporting goods store

An authorized boot dealer is one authorized by boot manufacturer(s); such dealers have a vested interest in gaining your confidence and respect, because they want your repeat business. As such, an authorized dealer will most likely have more time and expertise to share with you while you consider your purchase. The boot dealer may also be an active or former figure skater, having gone into the business for love of the sport.

You can locate the authorized dealer nearest you by contacting the boot manufacturers we have listed above.

Although mounting the blade to a new boot may appear easy (and there's many a "Tim the Toolman" ready to help you, with electric screwdriver tightly clutched in hand), it is a *very* exacting process, and we recommend that the procedure only be performed by *a qualified professional* (see Mounting and Sharpening Your Blades on page 9).

Purchasing through mail order, either directly from a manufacturer or through a retailer, has become extremely popular in the last few years. All you need is a phone or computer (if you order off the

Internet), and a credit card. Nothing compares with the convenience of having your boots and blades delivered right to your front door.

Mail-order retailers that deal in boots and blades usually run advertisements in skating magazines. Check to see if your local newsstand carries any figure skating magazines, such as *International Figure Skating*. Otherwise, you might want to request a sample copy of the magazine published by the United States Figure Skating Association (USFSA) and/or the Ice Skating Institute (ISI). Contact information is listed in chapter 6.

The downside of mail order is that it lacks the human touch. If your feet are hard to fit, you may find yourself shipping your boots back to the manufacturer or retailer. If you're not happy by the second or third try at a replacement, we recommend that you seek out an authorized dealer in your area. Dealers also have special tools and equipment that can help remedy any trouble spots (ankle pain, rubbing, sore spots) that may arise when breaking in your new skates.

Next-to-new sales hosted by skating clubs are generally held once or twice a year. Outgrown skates and skating dresses are usually the main offerings at a sale. When shopping at a next-to-new sale, look for boots that still retain some stiffness in the ankle area. Avoid boots that have deep creases or wrinkles in the leather, as these will not offer you the support your need. Pass by any boots whose tops tend to flop over.

When it comes to blades, light rust is okay, but avoid buying skate blades that are deeply gouged, nicked, or pitted.

Prices vary, but if you do find a decent used boot-blade combination, the seller may be willing to bargain. If unsold, any used equipment will only wind up on a hook in the basement or garage.

Bulletin boards at rinks may contain postings for used skates. If you find an advertisement for boots in your size that carry a brand name, it may be worth calling the number and setting up a meeting with the owner to inspect the skates. Apply the same standards for inspection we suggested for perusing skates at a next-to-new sale.

The obvious advantage of both next-to-new and bulletin-board shopping is that you can save a considerable amount of money. However, this matters very little if your skate size is not available and/or the quality and condition of the used equipment is not acceptable.

Your local sporting goods store may carry figure skates. Reidell and Don Jackson are frequently the brands stocked. New, both companies offer entry-level packages (boot *with* blade attached) for under $100.

The advantage of purchasing skates at a sporting goods store is convenience. Simply walk in with cash, check, or credit card, and walk out with your equipment. Also, if you encounter any product defect, your return is local and doesn't involve any shipping costs.

Realize, however, that sales staff in sporting goods stores may have little or no training in fitting figure skating boots and blades. They may lack the expertise and knowledge required to recognize the appropriate model for your level of skating. For the most part, sales personnel are generalists; they need to know a little about a lot—golf, tennis, basketball, football, baseball, hockey, and more.

As we mentioned earlier, if you progress in the sport you will eventually wind up buying a higher-end skate, and this means buying separate boots and blades. There are two major manufacturers of figure skating blades:

- Mitchel & King Skates, Ltd. (known in the literature as MK)
- John Wilson

Both companies are based in England, and both have an impeccable history of producing the finest blades ever to touch a sheet of ice. Products range from blades for beginners on up to those for the professional.

Blades may be available through your local authorized boot dealer. Mail-order retailers that sell boots usually also sell MK and Wilson blades.

Before we move on, let's discuss three more types of skates. Our message is clear and simple. Don't waste your time or money on:

- Any kind of "skate" that straps onto the bottom of a street shoe.
- Any kind of skate that has a double-runner (*two* pot-metal blades attached to the bottom of *one* skate). Double-runners give the skater a false sense of balance and security, the "blades" can't really be sharpened, and you'll wind up walking (more like "clacking") across an ice surface.

BLADE GUARDS

After your figure skates, the one piece of equipment that you absolutely *must* purchase is a pair of blade guards. Constructed of rubber or heavy plastic, blade guards come in a variety of designs and colors. Usually costing less than $10, they are the best investment you can make to protect your metal. Remember this rule of thumb: The *only* surface your blades should ever touch is a sheet of ice.

For us, hearing fingernails on a chalkboard is nowhere near as painful as the sound of someone walking across a concrete floor in skates *without* the blade guards on. That distinctive "crunch" is the sound of fine English steel being demolished with each footfall.

Wear your guards.

Even when you're just walking on the interlocking rubber mats used as flooring at indoor rinks . . .

Wear your guards.

- The kind of skates—usually purchased from a department or discount store for less than $20—constructed from plastic or vinyl one grade higher than Saran Wrap. These skates offer almost no ankle support, and the cheap metal blade often refuses to hold a sharpened edge.

Skate Care and Maintenance

We're going to assume that eventually you'll wind up buying your own skates. So let's talk about breaking them in, along with care and maintenance.

Breaking in Your Boots

Initially, your new leather boots are going to feel a little uncomfortable, so let's discuss the process of breaking them in.

Lace up your boots using the same procedure you use on a rental skate, then wear your skates around the house for 15 to 20 minutes at a stretch. (Be sure to wear your blade guards!) Forget about sitting on the couch watching TV; by "wearing" we mean engaging in *weight-bearing activity*. Standing, walking, and performing deep knee bends are all suggested for off-ice boot break-in. And if you're feeling really frisky, try dancing the mambo in your skates. (Just kidding!) But remember, your feet are elevated off the floor and balancing on a ¼-inch blade (encased in a blade guard, of course). Be careful!

During off-ice boot break-in, any mild discomfort in your feet will be offset by the swell of omnipotence you feel as you tower above (at least temporarily) all those in your household who used to call you "shrimpy." Feels great, doesn't it? All joking aside, the purpose of proper break-in maneuvers is to begin to mold the boot to your foot, soften the leather, and promote ankle flexion.

If you've purchased a midrange or high-end boot, most likely it will not come with a premounted blade. In this case walk only on carpeted floors to protect the leather sole. (Without the blade attached, you won't be as tall as a runway model, but the leather sole is quite slippery on rugs and carpeting. So again, watch your step.)

For really stiff boots, dampen your socks or nylons before placing and lacing your feet inside. It feels yucky, but it really does speed things along. (Don't worry about the leather inside your boot. It will dry.)

Have patience—the break-in process takes time, and it may be a while before you achieve comfort in your new boots. (Nikki says that she needs about six or seven house walks and the same number of sessions on actual ice before her new boots are tamed.) Remember, too, that *comfort* is a relative term. Skating boots are designed to grip your feet and ankles and keep them relatively immobile. Don't expect them to ever feel like your bunny-ear bedroom slippers.

Protecting Your Boots

If your boots have leather heels and soles (some beginner or entry models have molded black plastic bottoms), it is wise to apply a protectant to help prevent water damage. (After skating, you'll find that the bottoms of your boots and much of your blades are covered with melting ice.) There are a number of products on the market that are quite effective.

Patti swears by Whiltemore's Heel & Sole Enamel. Other skaters simply use liquid silicone waterproofing solution, which can be found on the shelves of most shoe stores. Still others will apply several coats of shellac to the entire surface of the boots' heels and soles, which gives the lower half of the boots quite a sheen.

Bernie uses both silicone *and* shellac. Nightly, he'll swab silicone on the heels and soles of new boots, using as much as the leather will drink. He'll go through an entire bottle (of silicone, that is), the process taking about a week to complete. Next, with an artist's brush, over the next several days, he'll lay on several coats of Bulls-Eye shellac.

Regardless of what product or method you use, make sure that you cover as much of the exposed leather as possible. If your blade is already attached to the bottom of your boot, simply work your brush or swab around the blade mounting plate.

Mounting and Sharpening Your Blades

As we stated earlier, blade mounting is a very precise process. You don't want to be skating on blades that are improperly set into the bottom of your boot. Your best (and safest) bet is to contact your nearest authorized boot dealer to have your blades mounted.

Once they're mounted, your local lawn-mower repairman or the clerk at the sporting goods store will be more than happy to sharpen your blades for you. But after all the time and money you've spent selecting proper equipment, are you really willing to risk your investment with someone not specifically trained to do the job?

Of course you aren't.

Most sporting goods store employees have been trained to sharpen *hockey* skates, which are rocked (curved or rounded) at both ends. Since a figure skating blade is straighter across, these folks just love to shave the heel and toe off your blades. (Patti can't remember how many times her students have come to her, in tears, with a "modified" figure skate, the blade having been newly altered compliments of the local sporting goods store.)

Local rinks may possess their own sharpening and grinding wheels, but do you really want to entrust your blades to a teenager who also doubles as the pizza maker at the concession stand?

Once again, we direct you back to your local dealer, a specialist in figure skating equipment. Fees and charges will range anywhere from $10 to $25 per sharpening, but you'll be pleased with the results, and the extra TLC from a skate professional will extend the life of your blades.

If you average one or two trips per week to the rink, your skates should be sharpened every six to eight weeks. Should you become completely addicted to the sport, quit your job, sell your house and car, and bicycle to the rink daily for six to eight hours of a grueling workout, then obviously your blades will need to go under the grinding wheel more often.

Daily Care of Boots and Blades

It is essential that you perform some maintenance on your boots and blades at the end of *every* practice session.

After removing your skates, take off the blade guards—skates should never be stored with guards on, because the accumulated moisture will create rust on the bottom of the blades. Wipe all wetness off the blades thoroughly with a soft, absorbent towel until the metal appears dry. To protect the blades during storage and to pick up any moisture you may have missed, slip on a pair of terry cloth blade covers (frequently referred to as soakers). These can be purchased at sporting goods stores or in skate shops.

Once you get home, remove your skates from the skate bag and place them in a well-ventilated area so that any perspiration captured within the boot has a chance to dry.

CLOTHING AND OTHER ACCESSORIES

Indoor rink temperatures can vary dramatically. You'll want to select clothing that you can layer (easily add or remove), covers all exposed areas, and has enough "give" so as not to restrict your movements. Although your local dance supply store or skating apparel shop may insist otherwise, you don't need to embark on your figure skating career dressed with the elegance of an Ekaterina, the pizzazz of a Petrenko. Save your money for good boots, blades, and timely sharpenings.

Sweatpants over long underwear or tights will work just fine. For your body core, wear a sweatshirt (not oversize!—which will hang too low and will restrict leg movements), or sweater over a turtleneck to keep warm and toasty. Pack a jacket or insulated vest in your bag just in case. A hat or headband (that can fit under a helmet) is recommended, and gloves or mittens are a must. Remember, it's better to be able to remove various articles of clothing than be underdressed and standing around shivering and stiff.

If your feet get cold, thermal booties that cover your boots will warm your toes nicely. You can purchase these from retailers who market boots and skating supplies, but hold off on your purchase until you've skated a few times and have concluded that you really need them.

Protective gear can help minimize initial skating fears and prevent the possibility of injury. We recommend helmets for every beginning skater, child or adult. It may look goofy, but a helmet will protect your noggin should it come into swift contact with the ice or the boards. A good, lightweight bicycle helmet will work just fine.

When you're at the sporting goods store (don't let them sharpen your skates!) to pick up a helmet, consider throwing in knee and elbow pads. We prefer soft pads with thick foam cushioning (as seen on basketball players) to those constructed of a hard plastic shell (designed primarily for in-line skating).

When skaters reach intermediate and advanced levels and start learning double and triple jumps, compression shorts—essentially spandex bike shorts with padding sewn into the hip and tailbone areas—are recommended. For now, you can mimic this effect by stuffing household sponges into the sides and back of your pants. Not a pretty sight, and your friends may think that you've put on a few pounds over the holidays, but the squares of sponge will help cushion any blows.

Older adult beginners may also want to consider wrist guards. When falling most individuals instinctively thrust out their hands to break the tumble. The hard plastic wedge sunk into the middle of a good wrist guard will take the brunt of the impact and prevent injury to your wrist.

Notice that we said "most." *Most* people stick out their hands when they fall, but we once watched Bernie perform a perfect belly flop onto the ice. At no time during his choreography did we see either arm move from his sides. He landed facedown, his lips pressed against the ice. He told us he was practicing Zen, kissing the ice, giving thanks and gratitude for its existence. We think that maybe he has a wire crossed somewhere deep within the recesses of his brain.

Now grab your skates (if you have them), or stick a few dollars in your pocket for rentals and session fees. You're ready for the next phase of your journey.

Let's go find some ice!

CHAPTER 2

ICE TIME

Eighty percent of success is showing up.

—Woody Allen

The more I practice the luckier I get.

—Anonymous

There are several different types of surfaces that you can glide on. Let's discuss some of the pros and cons of each.

LAKES AND PONDS

Pros

Free ice! The setting of a lake or pond is often as pretty and picturesque as a Currier and Ives print. The air is brisk and invigorating, and you can make like a husky, pulling your kids in a sled behind you. Perhaps best of all is the sense of expansiveness and freedom you'll enjoy in the great outdoors.

Cons

Ungroomed lake or pond ice is often rough, pebbled with bumps, and riddled with long cracks that will catch your blade and bring you down fast and hard. Stones, tree branches, and tree roots may be frozen into the ice and can wreak havoc with your sharpened edges. The guy pulling his toddler in a toboggan may be wearing his army boots, which leave a deposit of dirt with each step he takes. This dirt can hurt your blades. Because of uneven freezing and moderating temperatures, the ice is often thin in spots, and—just like you've seen on reruns of *911*—you could drop through. If you choose to go lake or pond skating, remember: No one is maintaining that ice surface except Mother Nature, so bring a snow shovel. You may have to clear off several weeks' worth of fallen precipitation. Lastly, you're limited to skating during the winter months.

GROOMED OUTDOOR RINKS

It's likely that the parks and recreation department of your city or town maintains a variety of outdoor rinks. The employees start by clearing and leveling an area of ground; when the weather turns cold, successive layers of ice build up. At night, after the skaters have gone home, workers will flood the ice with a hose, giving it a fresh surface that will be hard and slick by morning.

Some outdoor rinks *are* groomed by a Zamboni. If you ever have the opportunity to visit Lake Placid, New York, during the winter, for instance, make sure you skate on the Olympic Oval—the outdoor ice where Eric Heiden took five gold medals at the 1980 Olympics. (Bernie, fantasizing that he was Eric Heiden, once spent more than an hour at the Oval on a January eve when the mercury had dropped to −5 degrees. Although it took several hours and several stiff hot toddies to thaw him out, he walked around for days beaming and boasting of his experience.)

Pros

Again, you're outdoors. The surface is smoother than a lake or a pond, and you won't have to worry as much about gouging your blades on foreign objects in the ice. The hole made by the snowsuited youngster who sat for hours chipping away with the butt of his blade will be patched by a worker at the close of public skating hours. This way, if you're back on the ice the following day, you needn't feel anxious about falling into an opening roughly the size of your head.

Cons

Since the invention of the Zamboni—a large, square vehicle with four rubber tires, powered by batteries or propane, invented solely for the purpose of resurfacing ice—flooding has come to be considered rather archaic. Flooded ice still holds a fair number of bumps and imperfections. When the ice surface is really choppy, your blades will produce a noisy clattering sound, and your legs will receive an impromptu massage via the vibration. And on a bitter cold day, you may find yourself spending more time in the warming hut, fighting to stay warm, than you do enjoying the pleasures of skating.

INDOOR ICE RINKS

Pros

We admit we're biased: We want you to skate at an indoor rink. Nothing beats the convenience, the comfort, and the safety of indoor ice. A Zamboni is always used, the ice surface is smooth as glass, and there are rink guards and/or session supervisors who can curtail the antics of disruptive or dangerous skaters.

Cons

During peak times (usually public sessions held on winter weekends), indoor rinks can become so crowded it's like gridlock on a freeway—you literally can't move, stuck fast in human traffic. You'll wind up shuffling rather than skating. Get off the ice, go home, and do something else, because this sort of experience can quickly kill your enthusiasm for the sport.

READY, STEADY, GO!

Enough talk. Let's skate!

Your skates are on, properly laced. Now make your way to the edge of the ice. Remove your skate guards and set them down on the rubber matting next to the entryway. Step onto the ice. Take a deep breath in, and then exhale. Relax your shoulders, bend your knees slightly, tip your head up, and focus your eyes straight ahead.

BASIC SKATING POSITION

Now let's define your basic skating position. Adjust your legs so that they are slightly apart. Make sure your shoulders are directly over your hips. Position your arms so that they are a bit lower than shoulder height, elbows slightly bent and in front of your hips, palms facing down. Your chin should be up, with your eyes focused straight ahead. You should look like the illustration on page 17.

You're doing great!

Inhale deeply once again . . . then exhale. Imagine we're right there with you, giving you your own private lesson. Focus on keeping your weight over your skates. If your arms are slightly forward, this will minimize the risk of rocking your weight backward. Having your weight too far back on your blades could cause you to lose your balance and fall backward.

Check for other skaters, and then take three or four marching steps across the ice, each time lifting your blade to approximately ankle height. Rest. Put both feet together and feel the glide.

You're doing it. You're skating!

Take three or four more marching steps. Rest. Put both feet together. Glide. Repeat the cycle a few more times: March. Rest. Align feet together. Glide.

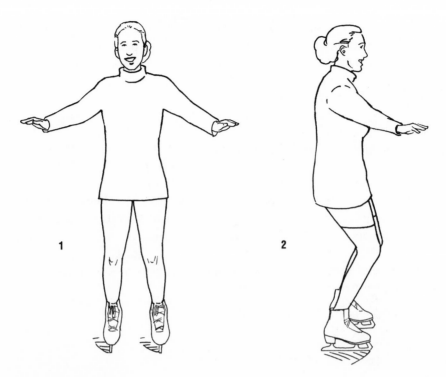

Basic skating position

Inside your skates you should feel pressure just slightly behind the middle of the bottom of each foot. This is to check that your weight is properly over your skates and your balance is correct.

Check your upper body. Make sure that your shoulders, due to excitement, haven't risen up to your ears, giving you the appearance of "Frankenstein on Ice." And keep breathing. You'd be surprised at how many beginning skaters hold their breath. As confidence is achieved, increase the number of marching steps between glides.

LEARNING TO FALL (CHOREOGRAPHED AND UNCHOREOGRAPHED)

Going Down

Should you feel the sensation of losing your balance, accept the fact that you're going into an *unchoreographed* fall. With this acceptance, try to relax as much as possible (your body will resist and attempt to fight the fall, putting you in awkward and ungainly positions), thrust your arms out in front, bend deeper into your knees. When you've almost touched the ice, lean sideways into the fall, so the impact will be cushioned with your thigh, butt, and hip.

See, you survived.

Now let's learn a *choreographed* fall—one you deliberately put yourself into.

To *make* yourself fall (sounds crazy, doesn't it?), stand with your feet apart, arms in front, palms down. *Lower* yourself to the ice by bending deeper and deeper into your knees. Again, when you're almost touching the ice, lean your weight sideways so your thigh, hip, and butt take the impact (see illustration below).

Learning to fall, choreographed or unchoreographed, makes you a better, safer, more confident skater. By looking your fear of falling dead in the eye, you confront an anxiety that prevents many people from ever attempting to skate.

Choreographed fall

Getting Up

Staying down on the ice too long presents a hazard to yourself and other skaters. Learn to get up quickly and efficiently. Here's how.

Technique A

Roll over onto your hands and knees, distributing your weight evenly. While keeping your hand away from the skate blade, lift one leg up so the bottom of the blade sits flat on the ice. Rock your weight forward so your hands bear most of your weight, bring your other leg up, set the blade flat on the ice, and roll your upper body into a standing position.

Getting up after a fall—Sequence A

Technique B

Again, start by rolling over onto your hands and knees. While keeping your hand away from your blade, lift one leg up so the bottom of the blade sits flat on the ice. This time place your hand on the knee you lifted, making sure your weight is shifted slightly forward. Place your free hand on top of your other hand and press down on your knee while simultaneously straightening your other leg. Roll up to a standing position.

Getting up after a fall—Sequence B

HOW *NOT* TO FALL

"Falling off the back of your blade" is the type of fall you really want to avoid. With a forward fall you've got your hands, knees, thighs, butt, and hip to cushion the blow brought on by gravity's pull. When you fall backward, your lower back and your noggin usually bear the brunt.

STOPPING

By now you're probably racing around the rink with wild abandon, crashing into innocent bystanders, grabbing the sleeves of other skaters in a frantic effort to slow down, or coasting to a stop and then hanging on to the boards for dear life.

Obviously, you do need to know how to stop. Here's how it's done.

Snowplow Stop

This is the most elementary way to bring your flow to a full and complete halt. Begin with your marching and gliding, but when you go into a glide this time, bend a little deeper into your knees and lean your boots inward so the inside edge of your blade starts to cut into the ice. Bear down on the entire inside edge of that blade, maintain your knee bend, and gradually press your legs and feet apart—but no farther than shoulder width (see illustration below).

You should be able to feel the sharpened metal biting into the ice, see a small spray of shavings coming forth around your blades, and hear a gentle skidding sound. Your snowplow marks the beginning of edge control; good edge control is critical to good figure skating. In the future you'll learn to position your blades so as to set or *catch* an inside or an outside edge—depending on what type of maneuver you're executing.

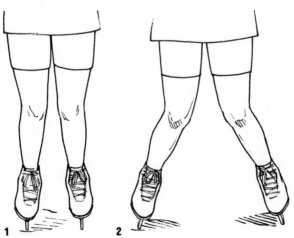

Snowplow stop

If you have difficulty bringing yourself to a full stop, Nikki suggests first turning your toes slightly toward each other (think a mild case of pigeon toes), then tipping your blades inward while applying pressure via the balls of your feet.

MORE BASIC SKILLS

The Forward Swizzle

In preparation for learning the forward stroke, you need to learn what's known in figure skating lingo as a swizzle. Here's how it's done:

Starting position: Assume the basic figure skating posture described and pictured on page 17.

1. Instead of beginning your marching steps, pull the heels of your boots together so they "kiss." (Look down at your feet—they should now be in the shape of a wide V.)
2. Bend deeper into your knees, and push your heels away from each other. Look down—your feet should now be parallel and shoulder width apart.
3. Now pull your toes in toward each other (think of two magnets attracting) while rising up slowly in your knees. As toes approach each other, draw your feet into a parallel position.

Throughout this and subsequent repetitions, both blades should remain in contact with the ice. If you can make out a tracing of your forward swizzle on the ice surface, it will have an oval-type appearance, like a lemon or a football (see illustration on page 23).

Let's do another.

Position your feet into a wide V, bend deep in the knees, and push the toes of your boots away from each other. Your feet are now shoulder width apart and parallel to each other. Draw your toes inward while coming up slowly in your knees.

Practice until you can do four or five swizzles in a row while building up speed, rhythm, and flow. At all times your blades should remain in contact with the ice, because the swizzle is a very fluid element. If a friend is watching, ask her if she notices a sinking and rising motion as you alternately flex and ascend in your knees.

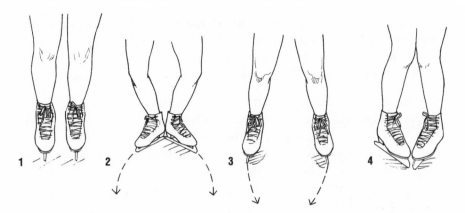

Forward swizzle

Remember, many of these movements may feel extremely foreign to you. Your muscles may resist, cramp, or clench—these are brand-new positions and movements for them. Learning to skate is a process. If you feel fatigued or frustrated, sit down, rest, and sip from your water bottle or refresh yourself with a hot cup of coffee or cocoa. Take a few deep breaths and be pleased with your progress.

The One-Foot Glide

In preparation for this figure skating element, we'd like you to step off the ice. Slip on your blade guards and walk to a relatively open area, a place where you can comfortably practice maintaining your balance on one foot only. (This will be your first taste of what's termed in the figure skating business as *off-ice training*.)

Position your upper body with your shoulders directly over your hips, your arms out a bit lower than shoulder height, and your elbows slightly bent and in front of your hips. Your palms should be down. Now lift the heel of one of your boots to the height of the calf of the leg that is supporting you. Keep the kneecap of the raised leg facing forward. Subtly shift your weight to maintain your balance as long as you can on your supporting leg. Keep your eyes looking straight ahead.

Resist the urge to hang on to the edge of a bench, snack table, or shoulder of the Zamboni driver.

Switch legs.

Balance off-ice until you start to feel a little muscle fatigue or terminal boredom. Rest.

When you're ready, get back onto the ice.

Starting position: Assume the prescribed skating position.

1. Take 5 to 10 marching steps, develop a good head of steam, and then align your feet together.
2. While gliding, slowly lift one foot a few inches off the ground, subtly shifting your weight so as to maintain balance on that one gliding skate as long as possible. Focus on a fixed spot straight ahead of you to help maintain proper body alignment.
3. Use your snowplow stop.

Repeat several times, alternating legs.

In Patti's experience, most people favor one gliding foot over the other. One just feels more natural, more stable, more comfortable. But continue to practice alternating your gliding feet so you develop ambidextrous legs.

Forward Stroking

Once you've grown comfortable gliding across the ice on two feet and then one, you're ready to move on to a more advanced form of forward locomotion. The fundamental pushing technique in figure skating is called the forward stroke. This maneuver will dramatically increase your power and flow on the ice.

To execute:

Starting position: Assume your basic skating position.

1. Place your feet so they form a T-position: one toe pointing straight ahead, the other foot behind and perpendicular. (The instep of your back foot should align with the heel of your front foot.)
2. Bend your knees. Press the inside edge of your back foot into the ice and push off, extending your back leg as you go. Push with the *entire length of the blade,* lifting your back foot so as to avoid pushing with the toe pick of your blade. (Toe pushing is a major figure skating faux pas.)
3. At the completion of the stroke, the leg you're gliding on (from here on to be referred to as the *skating leg*) should

remain slightly flexed; your push-off leg (from here on, your *free leg*) should stretch back fully extended and slightly to the side. Turn your free-leg foot out, point the toe, and keep it approximately 5 to 7 inches off the ice.

Now for the next stroke:

4. Draw your free leg in while rising slightly in your skating knee. When both legs are together, bend in your knees and shift your weight onto your free leg. When this weight shift occurs, the free leg *automatically* becomes your skating leg.
5. Push off with the inside edge of your *new* free leg, extending your leg back and out. (Again, you want a nice fluid push, using the entire length of your blade.)

Alternate free and skating legs and get a little mantra going inside your head. *P-u-s-h* and glide. Legs together. *P-u-s-h* and glide. Legs together. *P-u-s-h* and glide. Legs together. *P-u-s-h* and glide.

Backward Skating

Très cool.

Whereas forward skating requires your weight to be centered slightly behind the middle of the blade, backward skating will demand that your weight be over the ball of your foot. To find the ball of your foot, remove your skates and rise up on your toes. That pad you're resting on is the ball. If your weight is too far back on the blade you'll feel unbalanced and shaky; too far forward and you'll produce annoying scratching noises from the toe pick.

To begin, we want you to get accustomed to the feel of a backward glide. Find a free section of the boards (the wall that surrounds an indoor rink) and stand facing them. Place your toes about 4 or 5 inches away from the wall, feet parallel and shoulder width apart. Bend your knees until they line up with the front of your toe picks.

Take a quick look around to anticipate any traffic. Wait out any wild or squirrelly skaters who may be approaching.

Keep your head up and your eyes focused on a fixed spot in front of you. Place your hands flat on the wall, about shoulder height. Gently straighten your arms and release contact with the wall while maintaining your head position and deep knee bend.

Your weight will rock forward on your blades, so be sure to maintain a solid upper-body stability.

Practice pushing off the wall until you feel comfortable.

Self-Propelled Backward Skating

Push off from the wall and take a few small marching steps backward, toes pointed slightly toward each other, similar to your procedure for the forward swizzle. After about five or six steps, pull your feet together and glide. Coast to a stop, take a few more steps . . . and glide. Continue in this fashion across the ice, being mindful of your position in relation to other skaters.

Backward Swizzle

Starting position: Begin in your basic skating position.

1. Place your big toes next to each other and the heels of your boots apart. Bend your knees and push your feet farther apart, approximately to shoulder width.
2. Now start pulling your heels back toward each other (again, think of magnets attracting) while rising gently from your knees. Look down at the ice—lemons? ovals? footballs?
3. When your heels are an inch or two apart, draw your feet through the parallel position and on into the toes-together placement.

Begin again, performing several backward swizzles across the ice.

GENERAL REMINDERS FOR BEGINNING SKATERS

• Keep your head up, your shoulders back, and your hips underneath you. If you hear scratching noises, this indicates that you're leaning too far forward. Feeling unbalanced or like you're going to slip off the back of your blade means you're leaning too far back.

- Many of the skills you learned in this chapter are building blocks—the foundations for more advanced elements and techniques. As such take your time with them. You want your basic skills to be rock solid—your skating career built on cinder blocks, not sand.
- Skill acquisition is different for each individual skater, occurring on a varied schedule and timetable. Learning is influenced by your:
  1. Comfort level and level of relaxation
  2. Inherent sense of balance
  3. Level of fitness
  4. Amount of practice time
  5. Use of recommended equipment
- Dedication to and a love for the sport are more important than "talent."

CHAPTER 3

ONWARD

Our greatest glory is not in never falling, but in rising every time we fall.

—Confucius

FINDING YOUR OUTSIDE EDGE (NOT NEARLY AS DIFFICULT AS FINDING YOUR TV REMOTE)

Up until now your skating has been performed either on the flat of your blade (the area between the two sharpened edges) or on its inside edge. It's time now to head out on a quest in search of that gleaming *outside* edge.

If you're at an indoor rink, find an unoccupied or little-trafficked hockey circle. Hockey circles are usually colored red and reside in the corners and in the middle of the rink.

Place one foot firmly on the circle and the other outside it, parallel and about shoulder width apart. Orient your upper body toward the middle of the circle by rotating your chest a little less than 45 degrees. The arm *within* the circle should be placed behind you, palm down, fingers fully extended. The arm *outside* the circle should point in front of you, palm down, fingers extended.

Bend the knee of your skating leg (in this case the inside leg resting on the circle) and transfer your center of gravity to this leg, making it your primary weight bearer. Tip your skating-leg blade and boot slightly toward the inside of the circle while maintaining shoulder, hip, knee and ankle alignment.

You are now resting on an outside edge. Concentrate on where your body weight needs to be in order to have this outside edge remain set in the ice.

That's it. You're not going anywhere just yet. Simply concentrate on what it takes to keep that outside edge firmly set and biting into the ice, without any slippage in a lateral direction.

Now let's develop this into a true figure skating element.

THE FORWARD ONE-FOOT PUMP

Starting position: Find your outside edge, as described above.

1. While maintaining your upper-body position, draw your feet together. Generate a small amount of forward momentum by executing five or six marching steps, then glide with your feet together. Bend your knees, and remember to keep your weight centered over your skating leg.
2. Turn the toe of your other leg (your *outside* leg) approximately 45 degrees away from your skating foot. Apply pressure down into the outside edge of your skating leg by bending deeper into your skating knee.
3. Now, while simultaneously applying pressure to the inside edge of your outside skate, slide this leg out to shoulder width. This movement will propel you forward.
4. While maintaining blade contact with the ice, turn this foot in and draw it toward your skating foot. Rise gently in your skating knee while pulling your feet together (see illustration on page 31).

You should now be gliding forward around the circumference of the circle. Repeat the exercise until you've made it all around the circle. Stop, and then change direction.

The path of your outside skate will resemble a shallow letter C. Depending on your direction (clockwise or counterclockwise), the C will be forward (the way it is normally written) or backward. Make sure to practice this skill in both clockwise and counterclockwise directions.

Forward one-foot pump

BASIC FORWARD CROSSOVERS

It's easy to be dazzled by the sight of superstar skaters flashing around the rink—they're able to impress us by means of executing powerful forward and backward crossovers.

Once mastered, forward (and later, backward) crossovers will increase your speed and agility on the ice. Your forward one-foot pump is a prerequisite for performing a forward crossover, so learn it well.

When you're ready to move on, wander back over to your favorite hockey circle.

We'll start by familiarizing you with the sensation of crossing your feet while standing on the ice. Remember that your blades are longer than your feet, so you must be careful about clearance when you cross.

Starting position: Assume the same position on the circle as required for the one-foot pump.

1. Pick up your outside foot by lifting the knee and thigh. Keep your knee pointing straight ahead and your blade parallel to the ice.
2. Now *cross* your free-leg thigh over in front of your skating-leg thigh. Slowly lower your free leg down onto the ice, placing the foot solidly next to your other boot. (Be sure to place the entire blade down all at once. Touch down with your toe pick and you'll be taking a dive!)
3. Bearing weight solidly on the crossed foot, pick up your other foot and now bring it alongside your crossed foot (see illustration on page 33).

Repetition of this maneuver will not only teach you to walk sideways like a crab but also prepare you for the big enchilada—crossing over while gliding! When you're ready, drift back over to your circle.

Starting position: Start by placing yourself so you'll be traveling counterclockwise around the circle—your left foot on the color of the circle, your left arm in back, right arm in front.

1. Execute a forward stroke onto your left outside edge by pushing off and out with your right (outside) leg. Extend this leg behind you, keeping your skating knee bent.
2. Draw your outside leg straight in toward your skating leg, cross it over, then lower your boot down onto the ice, with its entire blade touching.
3. Shift your weight onto your right foot. Flex the toes of your left foot upward, lift the entire blade off the ice, and sneak it around the back of your right boot. Complete the action by pulling your feet together (see illustration). Make sure the movement of lifting the boot and blade is smooth and fluid so as to avoid hitting your toe pick into the ice.

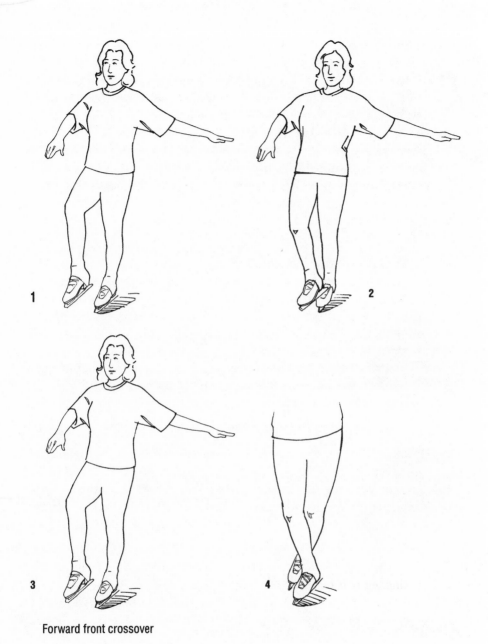

Forward front crossover

This is a basic, beginning crossover. Practice and become proficient in both directions around the circle. A more advanced version involves pushing with both feet.

TWO-FOOT TURNS

With this move you'll be learning how to turn front to back—forward to backward—while moving across the ice. Like many of the basic skills you're acquiring, two-foot turns act as a precursor for more advanced figure skating skills.

Here we go:

Starting position: Position yourself counterclockwise on a circle (circles, always the circles!). Your left foot should be on the color. Place your right arm across the front of your body, with your fingertips pointing toward the center of the circle. Extend your left arm in back of you, put your feet together, and bend your knees.

1. Look over your left shoulder.
2. Get ready, because you'll need to make two things happen simultaneously now: Swivel your hips to the left until your pelvis is pointed in the direction you're looking while also "checking" your arms. (To check, drop your arms, then snap them up over the circle.) Your right arm should now be over the circle behind your right-bun cheek, and your left arm should move across the front of your body with fingertips pointing toward the center of the circle.

Now let's perform the turn from a glide:

1. Take five or six marching steps and glide for a few moments.
2. Execute your two-foot turn while still in motion. Maintain your upper-body stability. Inside your boot, you should feel pressure rock from the back of the blade to the ball of your foot. You'll experience this sensation *only* inside your boot, isolated and without any upper-body movement. You should now be gliding backward, feet together, with your left arm in front and your right arm behind.

BACKWARD ONE-FOOT PUMP

Starting position: Go back to the circle. This time you'll be moving backward in a counterclockwise direction, so place your right foot on the color of the circle. Place your right arm behind you over the circle, slightly below shoulder height, palm down. Position your left arm in front and align the heel of your thumb with your belly button. Rotate your upper body slightly less than 45 degrees toward the cen-

HOCKEY STOPS

Want to learn how to cover other skaters with a light shower of ice and snow? It's done with a hockey stop.

Starting position: Start from a standstill, your arms out to your sides and slightly below shoulder height, and your eyes focused straight ahead. Place your feet parallel and approximately 1 to 2 inches apart, with your knees bent.

1. Briskly turn both feet a quarter turn, in either direction, while keeping them parallel. Your head, trunk, and arm positions all remain static. You should be able to feel the sensation of your hips rotating under your shoulders, and your weight should stay centered over your skates. Avoid leaning back; remember, falling off the back of your blade hurts.
2. At the end of the stop, your front foot will be angled onto an inside edge, and your back foot on an outside edge. Bear down into your edges to ensure a good bite into the ice (and a nice heady spray). The more pressure you apply to your edges, the more quickly and sharply you'll stop (see illustration).

If you've just had your blades sharpened, a hockey stop will be a little harder to execute, because your edges will bite faster. As some of that new edge wears off, the hockey stop becomes easier.

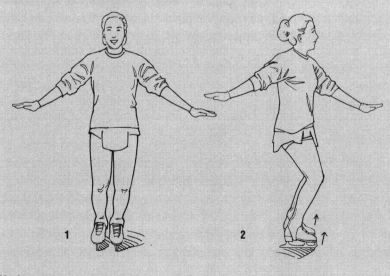

Hockey stop

Practice the stop from a standstill until you've eliminated any herky-jerky movements and feel relatively confident with the maneuver.

When you're ready, let's do a few from a glide:

1. Take five or six marching steps and progress into a glide.
2. Look straight ahead and fix on a stationary focal point. Bend your knees and keep your feet parallel.
3. With one quick movement, sharply turn your feet a quarter turn—in either direction—applying pressure equally into the ice with both blades. Maintain your knee bend and the parallel position of your feet.

With practice, speed, and some aggression, you'll be able to kick up enough ice to take revenge on the most obnoxious of ice rink patrons.

ter of the circle. Tip your chin up, and look back and beyond the tips of your right-hand fingers. With your knees bent, tip your right foot slightly onto an outside edge and shift your weight to this leg.

1. Pigeon-toe your left foot and turn the heel 45 degrees away from the right.
2. While pressing into the inside edge of your left foot, slide the foot out to slightly wider than shoulder width. Right knee should remain bent.
3. While maintaining blade contact with the ice, turn the heel of your blade back toward your right foot. With a slight rise in the knee, draw the foot in and through the parallel position. As with the forward one-foot pump, the path of your left leg will form a shallow letter C.
4. Repeat the procedure until you've made your way completely around the circle.

Once you're proficient, change directions so you're moving clockwise. This time your right foot will form the letter C.

BEGINNING BACK CROSSOVER

Once you master the backward pump, you're ready to advance to a back crossover.

Starting position: It's circle time again. Position yourself so you'll move counterclockwise. Your right foot should be on the color of the circle.

1. Develop some momentum by performing several backward pumps. While gliding backward on two feet, perform a single pump ending with your feet together.
2. Lift your left foot (with the blade parallel to the ice) high enough to clear your right (skating) foot. Cross your left thigh in front of your right and lower your left foot back down onto the ice, the entire blade angled onto a slight inside edge.
3. Shift your weight onto your left foot; then pick up your right, and sneak it around the back of your left. Bring both feet back to a parallel position.

Develop a rhythm—pump, lift, cross, together; pump, lift, cross, together; pump, lift, cross, together—traveling completely around the circle.

When you're ready, switch directions.

This is a beginning back crossover, incorporating both inside and outside edges, getting you acclimated to weight shifts from one foot to another while moving on a curve (whew!). As your technique progresses, you'll develop even more speed and cornering ability.

FORWARD OUTSIDE THREE TURN

With this nifty little element, you'll be turning from a foreward direction to a backward direction on one foot. You'll incorporate components of a two-foot turn and the back inside edge felt in the back crossover.

Go back and review the directions for a two-foot turn.

Most hockey circles have a red bull's-eye in the center. Because you'll need a tighter arc for this move, this time use a circle with a radius approximately 3 feet wider than the bulls-eye. The tighter arc will make it easier for you to feel both inside and outside edges of your blades.

Starting position: Position yourself about 3 feet from the bull's-eye with your left foot closest to the dot. You're heading forward in a counterclockwise direction. Your body, arm, and head movements will be identical to those you used in a two-foot turn. The only difference here is that a three turn involves only *one* foot.

1. March those five or six steps.
2. Pick up your right foot and bend the leg so you're holding your free-foot toe directly behind your skating-foot heel.
3. Press the calf of your right leg up against the calf of your skating leg.
4. Shift your weight over onto your left leg.

You should now be gliding forward on a left outside edge, and your weight should be slightly behind the middle of your blade. As usual, your skating knee should be slightly flexed.

5. As with the two-foot turn, you'll now make two things happen simultaneously. Your arms already have an inclination to the left, but you should increase that orientation now by applying pressure back to the left side of your upper body. Quickly release that pressure by checking your right arm behind your right buttock as your left arm comes across the front of your body and aligns with your belly button.
6. At the same time, snap your hips and buttocks half a turn so your rear end is now facing backward. You're now gliding backward on a left inside edge.

In the middle of the turn you should feel your weight rock forward onto the ball of your foot. You can facilitate this rocking sensation by rising gently in your skating knee while in midturn and sinking back down as your inside edge grabs the ice.

Keep your upper body positioned solidly over your skating leg during the turn, because any lateral movement will force you to drop your free foot onto the ice before you complete the maneuver.

Once you've put this element in your hip pocket, you'll have a way to change direction quickly and/or set up an entrance into a jump or a spin. In your skating career, you will encounter other types of three turns. A left forward outside three turn is just one of eight different varieties.

Take a breather. We've covered a lot of ice in this chapter.

Temper any frustration with patience and the knowledge that with each successive practice session, your mind and your muscles become programmed with the moves needed for fluid execution of these basic skating elements.

CHAPTER 4

THRILLS, CHILLS, AND *MORE* BASIC SKILLS

We can do anything we want if we stick to it long enough.

—Helen Keller

A s your repertoire of skating elements continues to grow, expect to feel a diminishment of your initial on-ice anxiety. It will be replaced by:

- The thrill of navigating yourself around the rink with an ever-increasing sense of enjoyment and confidence
- The anticipation and excitement of learning something brand new
- The knowledge that with each basic skill mastered, you become a more proficient and accomplished figure skater

THE T-STOP

It's a good idea to learn a nice repertoire of stops. You already know the snowplow and the hockey stops; now let's add the trusty T-stop into your bag of figure skating tricks.

continued

With this maneuver you'll be stopping using the *outside* edge of one blade while supporting yourself with the other. When properly positioned, your feet will actually form the capital letter *T,* with one blade pointing forward and the other perpendicular and behind.

First, let's practice the position.

1. Begin by placing your feet parallel, with your arms extended out to your sides, slightly below shoulder height, and a bit toward the front of your body; your palms should be down. Your shoulders should be over your hips, and your eyes looking straight ahead.

2. Lift one foot and place the instep of that boot directly behind the heel of the other, being very careful to *clear the back of the blade* of the boot facing forward. Your feet should now be formed into a capital *T.*

Check to see if your feet match the illustration.

3. Bend both knees and distribute your weight equally between your feet.

4. To catch the *outside* edge of your back boot (the top of the *T*), drop the outside of your ankle down toward the ice. This will essentially force the outside edge into the ice.

Remember to keep your knees bent throughout the entire execution of this skill.

Now let's do one for real . . . with motion.

Starting position: Since your feet are already in a *T,* you can start there.

1. Push out one stroke onto the blade that is facing forward, extending your free leg back behind you.

2. Gently bend the free leg into your skating foot, drawing your instep in behind your heel.

3. With the blade still poised in the air, begin to tip the outside of the ankle down toward the ice, and then gradually place the blade onto the ice. Both knees should remain bent.

4. Create the desired resistance by distributing your weight evenly between your two feet while the blade "skims" before finally grabbing the ice (see figure on page 41).

1

2

T-stop

If you do this correctly, you'll hear and feel the same distinctive skidding you heard and felt when performing your snowplow and hockey stops.

By bearing more weight on your back foot, the outside edge will skim for a shorter period of time as it takes hold in the ice. With newly sharpened blades, the T-stop becomes harder to execute, because the edge will grab quite quickly.

Remind yourself when you're positioning your back foot for placement on the ice to clear the back of your skating-leg blade. If you step down onto the back of this blade, you could be in for a fall. Again, backward falls are the hardest to break, with your back, butt, or head taking the impact.

Practice alternating free and skating legs. You'll find that you'll prefer one leg in front and the other in back.

Increase your speed only after you've achieved reasonable comfort and ability.

Thrills, Chills, and *More* Basic Skills

INSIDE MOHAWKS

Let's add to your skills base.

A mohawk is yet another way to turn from forward to backward, quickly and efficiently, while moving across the ice. Unlike the three turn which remains on one foot while turning, the mohawk actually changes feet as you turn. Similar to the three turn, there are a variety of mohawks used in skating.

Right Mohawk

To experience the movement path of the right mohawk, you'll need to practice at the boards.

Starting position: Stand with your *left* side closest to the wall and position your feet parallel. Orient your upper body toward the wall and place both hands on top of the wall, a little more than shoulder width apart. Your right shoulder should be leading.

1. While maintaining contact with the wall (by sliding your hands across the top), stroke onto your *right* foot, extending your *left* leg behind. Be sure to keep your right foot parallel to the wall.
2. Draw your free-leg heel perpendicular to and up against the instep of your right foot. At this moment, your free-foot blade is off the ice and your free-foot toe is pointing directly at the wall.
3. While continuing the forward glide, rotate your free-leg knee and toe so they point behind you while keeping your heel in contact with the instep of your right boot.
4. Turn your head to the left, so your upper body begins to facilitate the turning motion. Simultaneously, step backward onto your left foot and lift your right, extending it behind you.
5. You should now be gliding backward on your left foot, continuing to move in the same line of travel (see illustration on page 43).

Try this move several times until you are comfortable.

Why the wall?

The wall gives you fewer things to worry about while your feet are learning this pattern. Placing your hands on it stabilizes your upper body and encourages you to turn in the correct direction. When you're ready, stay close to the wall but lift your hands off it and perform the mohawk free-handed. Should you encounter an insecure moment, the wall can again quickly become your friend.

When you're *really* ready to leave the nest, give the wall a little tap to say thanks and good-bye, and mosey on over to one of the red bull's-eyes set in the center of a hockey circle.

Visualize the bull's-eye approximately 3 feet wider than in real life.

Starting position: Start from a T-position, your right foot leading, your right arm in front and left arm in back. Orient your upper body toward the center of the bull's-eye.

1. Stroke onto a right forward *inside* edge, gliding along the perimeter of the imaginary circle.
2. As you draw your free foot into your instep, feel your upper body rotate in the direction in which you are turning. Continue turning the free-leg knee and foot while at the same time turning your head to the left.
3. As you step onto the left inside edge and begin gliding backward, you should feel a subtle checking motion: Your right arm will check back to align with your new (right) free leg. Your left arm checks across your body so its fingertips are pointing in toward the bull's-eye.

Right mohawk

CONSECUTIVE FORWARD AND BACKWARD OUTSIDE AND INSIDE EDGES

Learning the following new skills will:

- Increase your mastery of edges
- Improve your flow across the ice
- Facilitate acquisition of more advanced skills (when that time arrives)

When performing consecutive edges, you will be executing a series of half circles across the rink using a red or blue hockey line as an axis (line). Most regulation-sized rinks have five hockey lines positioned across their widths.

Forward Outside Edges

Starting position: Begin by assuming a right T-position near the wall. Your right foot should be parallel to the wall, with the instep of your left foot placed directly behind your right heel. Your left side should be closest to the wall.

Position your right hand out in front of you, palm down and aligned with your belly button, your right shoulder leading slightly. Your left arm should be in back, but slightly out to the side.

As we mentioned, you'll be traveling in a series of half circles on either side of the red or blue line. It will be helpful to visualize those half circles as having a radius of about 4 feet.

1. Bend both knees and stroke onto your right forward *outside* edge. Flex your free leg in so that the big toe of your free foot is directly behind the heel of your skating foot. Rise gently in your skating knee.
2. To help maintain your outside edge, lift up on your free hip to keep your body more solidly aligned over your skating blade.
3. When you've covered half the distance of the lobe (the half circle), carefully sneak your free foot alongside your skating foot. Continue extending it until the heel of your free foot is directly in front of your skating-foot toe. The toes of the free foot should point directly over the imaginary half circle.

4. Upon completion of this movement, drop your arms to your sides and reverse their positions so your *left* arm and shoulder are now leading.
5. At this point, you should have done a complete half circle on your right outside edge and arrived back at the line. Pull your feet together, bend your knees, and push off onto your *left forward outside edge.* Repeat the process in the other direction. Continue in this fashion, zigzagging across the line until you've reached the other side of the rink.

Although this maneuver may sound simple, when you're actually on the ice you'll discover that it requires an enormous amount of upper-body control and precision in both arm and leg movements.

Forward Inside Edges

Starting position: Start in a right T-position, although this time your *right* side will be closest to the wall. Place your left hand in front and your right arm out to the side to form a sort of capital *L* position.

1. Bend your knees and stroke onto your right forward *inside* edge. While keeping your free-leg knee and hip turned out, bend your free leg and draw your toe in behind your skating-foot heel.
2. When you've reached the halfway point on the lobe, sneak your free foot alongside your skating foot and continue moving this foot forward until your free-foot toe is in *front* of your skating foot and its heel is next to your right (skating-foot) big toe. To maintain this inside edge, position and keep your free hip slightly down.
3. Once your free foot is in front, drop your arms to your sides and reverse positions so you are approaching the line with your right arm in front and your left arm out to the side (L-position).
4. Bring your feet together, bend your knees, and stroke onto your *left* inside edge. Be sure to push off of the right inside edge without using the toepick.
5. Repeat this process in the opposite direction and continue across the line until you reach the other side of the rink.

Backward Outside Edges

Backward edges are performed in the same pattern we described for forward edges.

Starting position: Begin at the wall with your left side closer to it. With your feet together, place your left hand in front, palm down, with its heel aligned with your belly button. Your right arm is in back and slightly off to the side. Your body should be slightly oriented toward the center of the rink and your head turned to the right, looking 2 to 3 feet beyond the fingertips of your right hand.

1. Bending both knees, perform a backward pump with your left foot while keeping your right knee bent. Upon completion of the pump, pick your left foot up directly in front of and in line with your skating foot.
2. When your foot comes off the ice, a subtle weight shift should occur. Make this happen by lifting up on your free hip as your foot leaves the ice, drawing your torso up tall and over your right leg. Keep your skating hip and shoulder in alignment. You should now be skating backward on your right outside edge.
3. At the halfway point on the lobe, bend your free leg at the knee and draw its toe directly behind your skating-foot heel. Keep your thighs pressed together to ensure that your free leg moves only from the *knee down*.
4. Drop your arms to your sides and reverse their positions, so your left arm is behind you and your right arm in front.

As you approach the line, turn your head to look over your left shoulder. Draw your feet together and bend your knees. You are now prepared to pump with your right foot, step onto your left back outside edge, and perform this skill in the other direction.

Continue across the line until you've reached the other side of the rink.

Backward Inside Edges

Backward inside edges are performed a bit differently than the three edges we just discussed. There is minimal arm movement, and the lobes can be slightly smaller.

Starting position: Begin by facing the wall with your arms out to your sides, slightly in front of your body, palms down. Place your feet together and flex your knees.

1. Slightly pigeon-toe your right foot so that the heel turns away from your left foot at a 45-degree angle. Tip your right-foot blade slightly onto an inside edge.
2. Now transfer your weight onto your right inside edge traveling backward while simultaneously performing a pumping motion with your left foot. Pick your left foot up directly in front of and in line with your right and rise gently in your skating knee. Bend your free leg, and pull the free foot back next to the skating foot.
3. Squeeze your thighs together and press down slightly in your skating knee.

Get ready, because we're about to introduce a new concept to you—*rotating your hips under your shoulders.*

4. To travel backward through the completion of the inside lobe, first turn your buns toward the line, then extend your free leg in the same direction, keeping your knee and hip turned out and rising gently in your skating knee. Keep your upper body as still and solid as possible. Your shoulders and chest should remain facing the wall. Focus your eyes on a fixed point straight ahead. Generally, if there is too much rotation in your upper body, you'll have difficulty maintaining your edge.
5. Your free leg will cross the line before the lobe is completed, so wait until your skating foot reaches the line before drawing your feet together, bending your knees, and repeating the entire process on your other foot.

That completes the instructions and information regarding basic skills. As we mentioned previously, your basic skills are your building blocks for more advanced and complicated figure skating elements (whether they be for freestyle or ice dance). Learn your basic skills well.

GENERAL REMINDERS

- Whether you're skating during a public session or one set aside specifically for figure skating, be aware. Always keep your head up and make a quick scan around your perimeter before attempting any of your basic skills. To rely simply on your peripheral vision or to believe that others are watching out for you because you're a beginner is foolish. Chapter 8 will discuss ice etiquette, protocol, and hierarchies, but for now, *skate defensively.*

- If you fall, get up quickly. A quick recovery from a spill helps ensure that parts of your anatomy won't get skated over by others on the ice.

- If you're beginning your figure skating career by skating *only* during public sessions (when the rink is open to everyone, and the skating fees are relatively low), try to arrive at the session early. Many times you can beat the rush of skaters who will pile in later. When skater gridlock sets in, attempting to practice can become extremely frustrating. Early-morning or lunchtime sessions at some rinks draw only a small number of participants. Take advantage of these. The more space you have, the more you'll be able to practice your basic skills fully.

- At some rinks, during some public sessions, figure skaters are relegated to a coned-in square or oval section at the center of the rink. If a rink guard (an attendant—usually identifiable by a bright jacket—hired by the rink to keep order and contend with any emergencies) sees you practicing anything other than forward stroking among the throng of other skaters (especially if the rink is packed), she might ask you to skate in the designated center section. Don't fight with her. Follow the rules of the rink. Again, attempt to seek out sparsely populated sessions, or purchase a specific figure skating "package" of ice time through membership in a club. We'll talk about this later.

- Should you decide to take group or private lessons, your skating coach may teach some of your basic skills differently than we have. Think of these instructions as a variation on a theme: same song, slightly different arrangement. There's no right or wrong here, just some stylistic distinctions.

Just think of how far you've come since your marching and gliding days!

And there are so many more good things to come.

CHAPTER 5

FREESTYLE

A strong passion for any object will ensure success, for the desire of the end will point out the means.

—Ben Stein

When you hand over your hard-earned cash for tickets to see this year's *Million-Dollar Superstars on Ice* tour, you're paying to see *freestyle*.

During the summer, when your friends are outdoors, boating, biking, and barbecuing, and you're indoors watching reruns of the 1992 Winter Olympics on cable, you're sacrificing your tan for *freestyle*.

And now, from this day forward, when family and friends ask you exactly what type of skating (hockey? speed?) you do when you head off to the rink, puff up your chest, pluck the tip of your toe pick, and proudly proclaim—*freestyle*.

That's right, you've lived through the blisters and, at times, the boredom of basic skills; now let's get you jumping and spinning like the big boys.

THE BUNNY HOP

We know: After all that buildup, "bunny hop" sounds a wee bit anti-climactic, doesn't it? But trust us, this is the best place to start.

(For all you macho guys, you can call it the rabbit leap if that makes you feel any better about learning it.) The bunny hop is an ideal beginning element for freestyle because it teaches you how to jump off the correct part of your blade.

Statistically, there are more righties (people whose right hand is dominant) on this planet. So, with all due apologies to lefties, our directions will be geared for right-handers.

A bunny hop is a lift off one toe pick and onto another, followed by an immediate change of foot. The change will be back to your original takeoff foot. You can begin by walking through the jump with one hand on top of the boards. For this first time there will be no incorporation of forward momentum, and no air time.

Starting position: Position yourself with your left side next to the wall and left hand resting on top of the hockey boxes. Extend your right arm to the side, slightly in front of your hip and a bit lower than shoulder level, with your palm down. Focus on a point in front of you.

1. Extend your right leg directly behind you while bending your left (skating) knee.
2. At this point two things will need to occur simultaneously: First, while rising in your skating knee, slowly swing your right leg forward. And second, as your right leg passes by your skating foot, stretch all the way up in your skating leg until you are standing up on your toe pick. Keep your right leg moving through until it extends in front of you approximately 8 inches off the ice. This will be the position from which you will jump.
3. For this static simulation, however, we'd like you to now step onto your right-foot toe pick, shifting your weight onto what is now your *new* skating leg. Immediately push off your (right) toe onto your left leg. Your left leg is, once again, your skating leg (see illustration on page 53).

Now that you've done the "still sequence," let's add a glide:

Starting position: Remain at the wall and assume the prescribed starting position.

1. Take a small stroke onto your left foot. From this forward glide, once again extend your right leg forward and push up onto the toe pick of your left foot.

Bunny hop

2. Immediately step down onto your right toe pick. As quickly as possible, push off from this toe pick onto a left forward glide.

At the completion of this moving simulation, you'll be traveling in a straight line down the ice on a flexed left knee with your right leg extended directly behind you.

Here's a little mantra that will help with this walk-through-with-a-glide: Kick . . . pick, glide. Kick . . . pick, glide. Kick . . . pick, glide.

Now for the real thing. Remember, it's named the bunny *hop* for a reason. You don't need to go barreling into this freestyle move with the force needed to jump the Grand Canyon. For the purposes of safety, remember:

- Head up, eyes straight ahead.
- Jump off the toe pick of your blade. (Jumping off the back of your blade could result in one of those nasty backward falls.)
- Keep your upper body stable.
- For your first several attempts, retain contact with the wall as you acclimate to the sensation of leaving Mother Earth.

Ready?

Starting position: With the left side of your body next to the wall, put your hand on top of the hockey box.

1. Stroke onto your left foot, making sure to bend your left knee.
2. Begin swinging your right leg forward. This time, however, as you rise up onto your (left) toe, *spring* gently off that toe pick, and alight briefly onto your right toe pick.
3. Quickly push off your right toe pick into a left-foot forward glide on a nicely flexed knee.

Repeat this exercise until you have established a comfort level. Then try the bunny hop without the security of the wall, gradually building your way up to several in a row.

Lefties should perform this drill in the opposite direction, with opposite footwork.

FORWARD PIVOT

A forward pivot is an artistic move used to interpret certain passages of music. It can also be used as a way to initiate rotational momentum as you enter into a two-foot spin.

Once again, these instructions are primarily directed to the right-handed skater. All jump-and-spin rotation for a right-handed individual will be in a counterclockwise direction. Conversely, a left-handed skater will rotate clockwise.

For all you "lefties" out there, when reading the instructions simply substitute right for left and left for right.

Starting position: Find a spot on the ice away from the wall where there is little traffic. Begin with your feet placed slightly more than shoulder width apart. Shift your center of gravity over your left leg.

To achieve this weight shift and move into a starting position:

1. Bend your left leg and slide your upper body in a lateral direction so your belly button aligns with your left thigh. Orient your upper body further to the left by exerting slight pressure back on your left shoulder. Your left arm should be back and slightly out to the side. Position your right arm in front with this hand aligned with your left hip. Turn your head slightly to the left.

2. Lift the heel of your left foot into the air so your weight *rocks* up onto your toe, forcing your toe pick to grip the ice.

To initiate movement of the pivot:

3. Tip your right foot onto a forward *inside* edge and begin a pumping motion with that foot. While your left toe pick is gripping the ice, the heel and knee of your left leg will begin to pivot *around* your left toe pick. Make sure that the momentum you gained by this pumping action is sufficient to keep your *right* foot even or slightly ahead of your anchored (left) toe.

4. While you're executing this element, your weight must stay in your left thigh. Keep your left hip in close alignment with your left shoulder and left knee. Maintain the bend in your left knee (see illustration on page 56).

A NOTE FOR LEFTIES

Many coaches actually teach a lefty how to skate right-handed. Their reasoning is that in the long run, this will make it easier for the skater: Left-handers are constantly fighting traffic in crowded freestyle sessions. If you are left-handed, we suggest that you be evaluated by a skating coach to see in which direction—clockwise or counterclockwise—you appear to jump and spin more easily and proficiently.

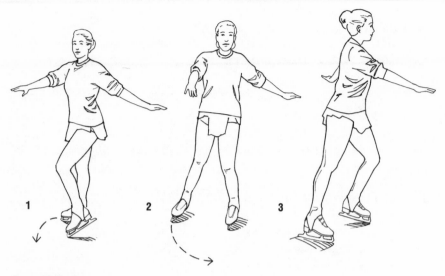

1   2   3

Forward pivot

As you become more proficient with the motor skills needed to perform the pivot, elongate the pumping action so the rotation becomes smoother and the pumping less obvious to the eye.

THE TWO-FOOT SPIN

Welcome to the wonderful world of spinning! A two-foot spin offers you an excellent introduction to this world, and accustoms your brain to rotational input.

Starting position: Lower-body-wise, the two-foot spin starting position is identical to that of the forward pivot—your feet slightly more than shoulder width apart, your weight over your left thigh, your left blade rocked up onto that toe, and your toe pick gripping the ice.

However, your upper body should be twisted to your right, away from your left toe. Your right arm and shoulder should press back behind you, slightly lower than shoulder height. Your left arm should come across your body, with its fingertips pointing behind you. Turn your head back toward your right shoulder. The idea here is that you're winding up your torso like a spring or propeller to initiate the momentum for the spin.

With upper and lower body in the prescribed positions, you've struck your starting pose. Now let's make the spin happen:

1. Bend both knees equally. With your arms held taut, *uncoil* the spring by snapping your arms around and to the front so that they are directly in line with your shoulders.
2. As you snap your arms, stretch up in your knees, straightening both legs and planting both blades on the ice, feet parallel.

The force of these two coordinated movements will initiate the beginning rotation of a spin, but now you'll need to increase the speed of your spin. Here's how:

Two-foot spin

3. While maintaining tautness in your arms, draw your elbows into your rib cage and cross your arms in front of your chest. (Retracting your arms cuts down on wind resistance.)
4. At the same time you're pulling your arms inward, draw your feet closer together. Here you have two choices for foot position:
   - Draw your feet into a parallel position approximately 2 to 3 inches apart.
   - Draw your toes together in a pigeon-toed stance (see illustration on page 57).

   Experiment, because one of these two positions will feel more comfortable and work more effectively for you. (Pulling your feet close together results in smaller, tighter circles and the desired increase in speed.)

Dizzy? All skaters, to a lesser or greater degree, experience dizziness when they spin. This is quite normal. It may take some time for your movement systems to accommodate and adjust to this type of movement. Pace yourself. If you start to feel nauseous or disoriented, take a break. Work on some other element, go sip some water, take a few laps around the rink. Come back to the spin when the world settles down.

THE FORWARD LUNGE

A lunge is an accent move—one usually incorporated into the choreography of a skating routine for the purposes of highlighting a specific passage of music. It can be combined with various types of arm movements in order to interpret different tempos and rhythms.

We'll start your lunge without any forward momentum.

Starting position: From a standstill, place your feet in a T-position with your left foot leading (the right is just as acceptable). Arrange your upper body into a basic stroking position—chin up, shoulders relaxed and directly over your hips, arms extended slightly lower than shoulder level and a bit in front of the hips, palms down.

1. While keeping both feet on the ice, begin bending your left knee, slowly *sliding* your left foot straight ahead while transferring your center of gravity to your left thigh. To achieve this weight shift, press your belly button out over

Forward lunge

your upper left thigh while maintaining an erect upper-body carriage and a slight arch in your back.

2. At the completion of the position, your left knee will be *deeply* bent, with its kneecap pushed out over your left toe. Your right leg will be fully extended, with the inside of your right boot actually resting on the ice, blade up and off the ice. To ensure proper form, keep your feet perpendicular (see illustration above).

Add some lead-up forward momentum and your lunge is complete and ready for performance.

The Forward Spiral (Arabesque)

Say the word. *Arabesque!* Notice how it just rolls off your tongue, so elegant, so mysterious, conjuring the most exotic of images. Unfortunately, these days it is most often referred to as a forward spiral—not to be confused with what a quarterback throws. But remember the older terminology when you execute this freestyle element, because it is a gorgeous artistic move used in the interpretation of passages of program music.

Although there is a simplicity to the spiral—in contrast to triple and quadruple jumps—many variations can be performed. Spirals can be on different edges; they can feature different free-leg positions, and different arm and upper-body positions. Executed well, a spiral can display drama and be quite eye catching for judge and spectator alike.

Eventually you'll want to be able to perform spirals on either edge, either leg, and both forward and backward. But let's start you off gliding forward in a straight line on your left foot, with your right leg extended behind.

Starting position: At the hockey box, position yourself in a T, with your left foot leading, parallel to the wall, and your left hip closer to the wall. Secure yourself by gripping the top of the box with your left hand. Extend your right arm directly out from your right shoulder.

1. While keeping your chin up and eyes focused straight ahead, bend slightly forward from the waist and align your belly button out over your left skate. At the same time, *elevate* your right leg behind you while maintaining the turnout in your hip, knee, and foot that is derived from the T-position. "Lock" both knees and point your free-foot toe. The heel of your right boot should align with your left bun.
2. Pull your shoulders back and put a generous arch in both your upper and lower back. The desired body line from the top of your head to the tip of your right toe should resemble the two ends of a banana pointing upward.
3. Keep your supporting leg totally straight and maintain pressure (inside your skate) over the heel of your left blade. This prevents you from rocking onto your toe pick when you glide forward.

Before venturing out into open spaces, glide parallel to the wall while allowing your left hand to slide along the top of the hockey box. Determine when you're ready (and if rink traffic permits), and then skate out to a free area on the ice.

1. Perform two or three forward strokes.
2. While keeping your eyes, chin, and upper body pointing straight ahead, slowly and with an even rhythm begin lowering your stomach and elevating your right leg behind you. Lock both legs and extend your arms out from shoulders, palms down, fingers extended.

Lifting your free leg higher contributes to dramatic effect (see illustration below).

Lastly, speed is an essential element in executing the spiral. Too little may result in a loss of balance; too much and you're out of control. And always, always be aware of your proximity to other skaters before elevating that free leg.

Spiral

ROTATION JUMPS

With the exception of the bunny hop, figure skating jumps involve rotation. Jumps fall into two categories: *edge jumps* and *toe jumps*. The difference is the way you launch into the air.

With an edge jump you travel on an edge (a curve) and launch directly into the air from that edge. There is no assist from your other foot. Edge jumps include:

- Waltz jump (takeoff from a forward outside edge)
- Salchow (takeoff from a back inside edge)
- Loop jump (takeoff from a back outside edge)
- Axel (takeoff from a forward outside edge)

Performing a toe jump involves a launch that incorporates an assist from the toe pick. Begin the jump by gliding backward on one foot. At the correct moment you'll reach back with your free leg, press your toe pick into the ice, and vault into the air. Toe jumps include:

- Toe loop
- Flip jump
- Lutz

The Waltz Jump

A waltz jump begins with a forward outside edge takeoff, rotates half a turn in the air, and lands on the opposite foot gliding backward on an outside edge.

Sound complicated? Not to worry. As with most of the maneuvers in this book, we'll break it down into bite-sized pieces for you. Again, instructions will be presented in a right-handed format. Lefties should just reverse directions.

The waltz jump, similar to the bunny hop, will involve rocking your weight from the entire blade onto the toe pick. Let's learn some lead-up drills first:

Starting position: Stand with your feet 3 to 4 inches apart. Position your left arm in front, straight out but slightly lower than your left shoulder. Glance down and imagine a clock lying on the ice. From this perspective, your left arm would be at 12 o'clock. Now place your right arm at 4 o'clock. Turn your hands so your palms are facing down.

1. Bend both knees. Look straight ahead and, while keeping your upper body erect, rock your weight onto your toe picks and gently spring straight up. Point your toes while in the air so they'll touch down first on the landing.
2. As your toe picks hit, simultaneously bend your knees and let your blades rock back down onto the ice.

Repeat until the motions are fluid and you're comfortable with jumping on the ice.

Now let's add the rotation:

Starting position: Assume the previously described position, but this time make sure your toes are pointing toward one of the rink walls (dasher boards).

1. As you begin to jump, *snap* your hips in a counterclockwise direction.
2. Upon completion of the jump, you will have rotated half a turn, and your toes will be facing the opposite wall.

Make sure to:

- Keep your knees bent on both takeoff and landing.
- Jump off your toe picks.
- Maintain proper upper-body and arm positions (don't rock forward or backward).
- Keep your eyes straight ahead and your chin up. (We know of one coach who yanks on the ponytails of her students when their heads start to droop. It's a bit mean spirited, but effective.)
- Relax. Breathe. If you hold your breath—and some students do—the mind interprets this as an alarm and tells the body to tense up.

Once you've got this lead-up procedure in your pocket, you can add a small amount of forward momentum:

Starting position: Find your favorite red hockey circle and position yourself with your left arm in front and right arm in back (12 and 4 o'clock).

1. Generate a minimum amount of speed by taking several marching steps.
2. Glide.
3. Perform the jump with the rotation from this two-foot glide, making sure to follow the arc of the circle.
4. On landing, you must rock from toe to blade *quickly* in order to flow backward out of the jump.

Once you've mastered the two-foot jump, it's time to move on to a one-foot takeoff:

Starting position: Stay right there on the hockey circle, only this time place your feet in a T-position with your left foot leading. Your arm position remains the same—12 and 4 o'clock.

1. Stroke onto a left forward outside edge while simultaneously stretching your right leg and both arms behind you. Although both arms are back, your left shoulder should be leading into the jump. Your eyes should look straight ahead and slightly to the outside of the circle.
2. Begin swinging your right leg and both arms straight through (your arms will pass close to your body and then forward).
3. As your free leg passes next to your skating foot, press up onto your toe and launch into the air.
4. As your free leg continues to extend forward, snap your hips around, pull your feet together, and land backward on both toe picks.
5. Immediately rock back onto your blades so you're gliding backward on bent knees. Return your arms to the 12 and 4 o'clock positions (see illustration on page 65).

Four factors will assist you in achieving more loft:

- The springing action from your left thigh, knee, and ankle
- The extension and lift-through with your free leg
- The added impetus supplied when your arms swing straight through from back to front
- Maintenance of an erect upper-body position

Feeling lucky? Let's go for a one-foot takeoff *and* a one-foot landing.

1. This time as you extend your right leg through and jump, shift your body out over that leg and land backward on the right outside edge on a flexed knee.

2. Fully extend your left leg directly behind you, with the hip, knee, and toe turned out so that the heel of your left boot is aligned with the heel of your right boot. To maintain that back outside edge, make sure your upper body is stretched tall directly over your right leg and the free (left) hip is lifted up.

3. An elegant landing position will finish your waltz jump in style—chin up, shoulders relaxed, back slightly arched, your free leg fully extended with its toe nicely pointed.

Waltz jump

Once you're proficient at this, you will have mastered the waltz jump in isolation. But most frequently this jump is performed from back crossovers. Here's how it's done:

1. Execute two or three back crossovers in a counterclockwise direction (the number can be increased as you become more expert).
2. Pull your feet together, and then pick your left foot up, and place the toe directly behind your right heel, keeping your thighs together and knees close. Stretch your upper body tall over your right leg so you are riding on a slight back outside edge.
3. Drop your arms to your sides and *switch* their positions so your right arm is at 12 o'clock and your left at 7 o'clock.
4. Turn your head and look behind you in the direction you are about to step.
5. As you stroke forward:
   - Drive down into your left knee and extend your right leg behind.
   - Stretch both arms behind you, but keep your left shoulder slightly in front.
   - Look straight ahead—*not* over your left shoulder. Keeping your head straight will ensure that the jump lifts first and then rotates.
6. You're now ready to jump, so . . . go for it!

The Half Flip Jump

The half flip will be your first toe jump. It begins from a back inside edge, vaults off the opposite toe, rotates counterclockwise half a turn, and ends gliding forward. (A full turn is 360 degrees; half a turn constitutes 180 degrees.)

The back inside edge leading into the half flip can be attained from either a right mohawk or a left forward outside three turn. However, in the interest of keeping your takeoff in a relatively straight line (the most effective strategy for a toe jump), we recommend beginning with the right mohawk.

First, perform a walk-through of the movement sequence at the wall:

Starting position: Sidle up to your old pal the hockey box and position yourself in a right T with your left side closest to the wall. Place your right hand flat on the wall in front, your left hand on the wall in back.

1. Push onto your right foot and perform the mohawk.
2. As your right foot leaves the ice, extend it directly behind you with the toe slightly turned out and about 2 or 3 inches off the ice. Be sure to keep your hips square. Simultaneously, bend your left knee.
3. With your right leg extended, firmly grip the ice with your right toe pick. (Make sure that your right ankle is strong, because you will be bearing weight briefly on that foot.)
4. At the same time, begin to bend your right knee and draw your left leg back toward your right toe.
5. As your left foot approaches your right, pick it up so you are now standing on that right toe (see illustration below).

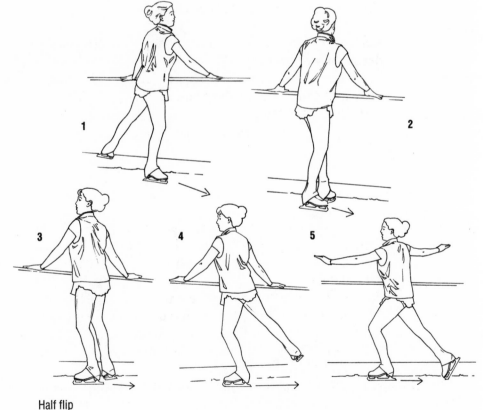

Half flip

Half flip (continued)

This is the position from which you will jump. From here on you'll need to release your death grip from the wall, but keep your left arm in front and the right in back.

6. To initiate rotation, snap your rear end toward the wall (counterclockwise) and vault off your right toe. Rotate half a turn in the air and land forward on your left toe. Immediately step into a forward glide on your right inside edge with a flex in your right knee.

7. On landing (just as with the takeoff), your left arm should be in front. Your right arm, upon landing, should be in back but a bit more out to the side (see illustration above).

When you're comfortable, try moving away from, but remaining parallel to, the wall.

It's important that after the mohawk, your left arm is positioned directly in front of you and your right arm straight in back. Keep your eyes looking straight forward as you draw your left foot back. (Again, this ensures that the lift *precedes* the rotation.)

Tap gently with your right toe. The objective with a vault is to launch *up* off the ice, not dig a trench down into it. If you find yourself digging deep holes in the ice, reexamine your right-leg extension after the mohawk. High kicks score points in Karate but not in freestyle figure skating. Your technique will suffer, and so will the Zamboni driver who will have to repair the damage made by your "donkey kicks."

The Half Lutz

The half lutz is another half-turn (180-degree) toe jump that closely resembles the half flip. Spectators and skating judges alike frequently have difficulty discerning which jump is the lutz and which is the flip. Whereas the approach to the half flip is made from the back inside edge, the entry edge into the half lutz is a back outside. This increases the difficulty of the jump, because you perform the rotation in the opposite direction of the path of your entry edge. (The back outside entry edge will be curving in a clockwise direction; after you plant your toe pick and jump, you will rotate counterclockwise.)

The takeoff for the half lutz is approached from back crossovers performed in a clockwise direction (right foot over left). We'll divide the actual setup for the jump into five clear steps.

Starting position: Perform three or four clockwise back crossovers to build a moderate amount of momentum. Position your right arm in front, in line with but slightly lower than your right shoulder. Your left arm should be in back and slightly out to the side. Pull your feet together so you're gliding backward in a straight line on two feet.

1. Execute one back pump with your right foot.
2. Lift up your right foot in front of your left with its heel directly in front of your skating-foot toe.
3. Bend your right leg at the knee and bring the toe pick of that foot directly behind the heel of your left boot. Although your right knee is flexed, keep your knees together. Your direction of travel should still remain backward in a straight line on the flat of the blade.

4. Drop your arms to your sides and reverse their position so the left is now in front, with the heel of your hand in line with your belly button. Your right arm should be straight behind you, in line with your right bun cheek.
5. Bend your left knee. Rock from the flat of your blade onto your back outside edge. Achieve this by elevating your free (right) hip and drawing up through your ribcage and chest so your entire body is oriented up tall over your left leg. Your eyes should be focused on a point straight ahead (see illustration below).

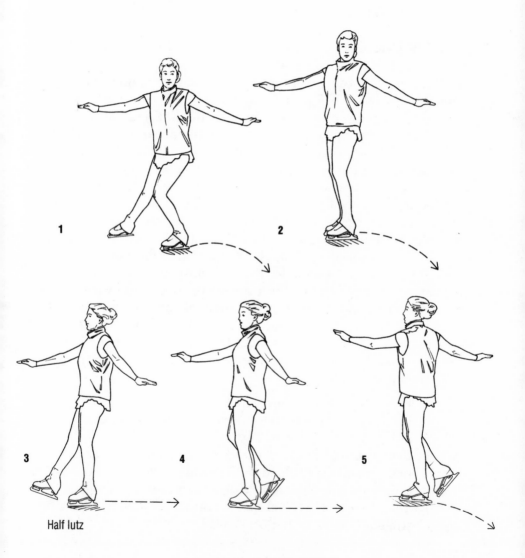

1

2

3

Half lutz

4

5

You are now in the perfect position to perform the half lutz.

1. While maintaining your left-foot outside edge, extend your right leg directly behind you with its toe pointed and ankle strong. Firmly grip the ice with your right toe pick. While beginning to bend your right knee, draw your left foot back toward the right.
2. As your left foot approaches the right, pick it up in front by lifting up on your left knee and thigh. You will bear weight briefly on your right toe before *vaulting* off it, rotating 180 degrees to the left by snapping your hips in a counterclockwise direction.
3. Land on your left toe and instantly push off that toe into a forward glide on your right foot with the right knee bent (see illustration below).

As you may be able to see, the motor sequences of the half flip and half lutz are remarkably similar—thus the common confusion

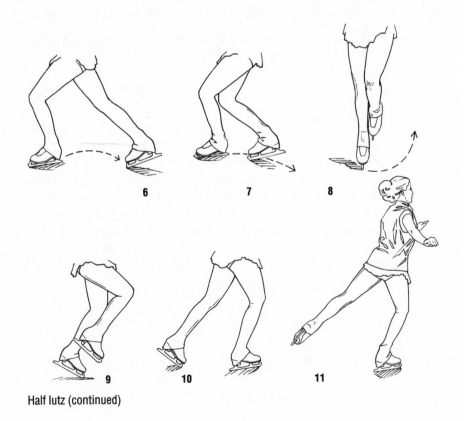

6   7   8

9   10   11

Half lutz (continued)

between these jumps. Television commentators will often refer to an incorrectly performed lutz as a "flutz," indicating that the skater failed to achieve the outside edge on the lutz takeoff.

The Toe Loop

The toe loop is the first full-rotation (360 degrees) jump you will learn. Your approach to the jump will be from a back outside edge of one foot and a spring off the toe pick of the other. The jump rotates counterclockwise; you'll land on a back outside edge with your free leg extended behind you.

Commonly, the back outside edge entrance to the toe loop is achieved by performing a forward *inside* three turn. This three turn is executed in a fashion similar to the forward *outside* three turn—a move you've already learned (see page 37).

Starting position: Begin in a T-position with your right foot leading. Position your right arm at 12 o'clock, slightly below shoulder height, palm down. Put your left arm at the same height at 7 o'clock.

1. Stroke onto a gently curving forward inside edge and bend your free leg *in* so that its toe draws in behind your skating-foot heel.
2. Simultaneously bend your right knee and bring your right arm across your chest.
3. While keeping your legs together, snap your hips around in a counterclockwise direction while releasing the cross pressure on your right arm and performing a checking action. Checking should create a reversal of your arm position so that upon completion of the turn, you will be gliding on a back outside edge with your right arm at 5 o'clock and your left in front at 12 o'clock; the heel of your left hand should be aligned with the middle of your chest. Your legs remain together, and your upper body will be oriented up over your right leg (see illustration on page 73).

The toe loop is a toe jump and therefore travels in a relatively straight line. Also, with this jump the forward and backward edges of the three turn will be marginal.

Practice the three turn until you've arrived in your comfort zone. Once comfort is achieved, head to a hockey box so you can walk through the sequence of the jump.

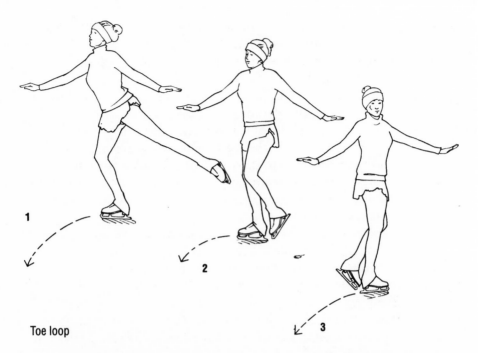

Toe loop

Starting position: Let's pretend that you have already done the right inside three turn next to the wall. Your right hip will be closer to the wall. You'll be standing on your right foot with your legs together, the left one slightly bent with its toes directly behind your right foot and pointing down toward the ice. To help maintain your balance when learning the sequence of this jump, rest your left hand on the boards in front of you and place your right hand on the wall in back of you.

1. Bend your right knee and begin extending your left leg directly behind you, keeping your hips square. Once this leg is fully extended, its toe should be pointed down and elevated 3 inches from the ice. Your kneecap will be facing down, with your ankle taut and in alignment with the rest of the leg.
2. Grip the ice with your left toe pick, bend your left knee, and begin sliding your right foot back on the *outside* edge. Because your right foot must maintain the outside edge as it draws back, you will actually be drawing the heel of your blade back on a diagonal so that it will travel *across* in front of the left toe.
3. When your right blade is about 6 inches away from your left toe pick, you'll need to do three things at once:

Freestyle

- Release your left hand from contact with the wall, but keep the arm in front at 12 o'clock.
- Shift your body weight back and actually stand on your left toe pick.
- Lifting your right foot with its heel leading, draw the foot across in front of and beyond your left leg. (As your right leg continues to move, it will cross in front of your left thigh.) From here the leg should thrust through behind you and slightly to the side with lift and extension similar to those in the waltz jump.

4. To complete the jump, simultaneously spring off your left toe pick, snap your hips and buns in a counterclockwise direction, let go of the wall, and land backward—first on your right toe, and then immediately pressing the blade down onto the ice. Upon completion of the jump, your left leg should be fully extended behind you, turned out from the hip. You may notice that this landing position is identical to that of the waltz jump. Your arms will remain the same on the landing as they were on the takeoff: left arm in front, right arm in back and slightly out to the side. (If necessary, you can put your hands back on the wall for the landing.)

TOE LOOP REMINDERS

The power for the jump should derive primarily from your lower body. Twisting your trunk or head to facilitate rotation will actually cause the jump to spin around instead of lift off. (This will be true for all your jumps.)

To maximize loft in this jump:

- Keep your left arm in front on takeoff.
- Look straight ahead as you draw back.
- Keep your weight oriented toward the right side for as long as possible while you are drawing back.

Now that you are familiar with the particulars, we'll add the three turn and a small amount of forward momentum. So go find a relatively uninhabited section of the ice.

Starting position: Start in a T-position with your right foot leading.

1. Stroke onto the inside edge and execute a three turn.

Toe loop (continued)

2. From the back outside edge, extend your left leg (with toe and kneecap pointed down) directly behind you.
3. Once your toe pick is planted, it is essential that you draw your right leg back and across the left and kick it through as quickly as possible. (This will prevent a "toe waltz jump"—a major faux pas thus called because the skater pivots on the left toe before jumping, causing some of the rotation to occur on the ice instead of in the air.)
4. The landing of the toe loop is on a secure right back outside edge with your skating knee bent. Perform an elegant extension behind you, with your free leg, chest, and head held high (see illustrations on pages 73 and 75).

The Salchow

The Salchow takes its name from skater Ulrich Salchow, the inventor of the jump. When spoken it sounds like *sow cow*. Sometimes the *cow* is left off, as in: "Sadly, Kristi fell on her triple sal [*sow*]." Would have been a lot easier if his last name was Smith or Jones.

In any event, the Salchow constitutes your first full-rotation *edge* jump (the toe loop was your first full-turn *toe* jump). The Salchow takes off from a back inside edge, turns 360 degrees in the air, and lands on the opposite foot . . . gliding on a back outside edge.

The usual entrance into the Salchow is from a left forward outside three turn. Occasionally some skaters enter from a right mohawk.

Starting position: Form a T-position with your left foot leading. Your right arm is placed in front at 12 o'clock, with its hand straight out from your sternum. Position your left arm behind at 7 o'clock with its hand aligned with the top of your left bun cheek.

1. Push onto a left forward outside edge with your skating knee bent and your free leg extended behind you and lifted. While maintaining the free-leg extension, perform the outside three turn.

If executed properly, you should now be gliding backward on a left inside edge, free leg extended behind, left arm in front and right arm in back.

2. Bending your free leg slightly, smoothly pull it in toward your skating leg so that your right thigh is slightly ahead of your left leg and the instep of your right boot is 4 to 6 inches in front of your left big toe. Slightly pigeon-toe your right foot.

3. Keeping your left arm in front, deepen the back inside edge by pressing farther down in your skating knee and turning your back and hips slightly more into a counterclockwise direction. Now simultaneously deepen the curve of the back inside edge, straighten your free-foot toe (out of the pigeon toe), and thrust your right foot and leg back behind you and slightly out to the side. As the leg thrusts through, vault up off your left toe pick, snap your hips counterclockwise, rotate 360 degrees, and land on that now-familiar right back outside edge (see illustration below).

Notice that your landing is the same as on both your waltz jump and your toe loop.

1   2   3

4   576

Salchow

ESSENTIALS FOR THE SALCHOW

- You must firmly check your three turn with your arms and shoulders. This prevents the jump from spinning off the ice. For the same reason, make sure that on the three turn, your free leg remains relatively motionless. Allowing it to swing wildly during the turn will diminish your control over the jump.
- The movement of your free leg from back to front must be purposeful and deliberate. This form of "committing" to the jump contributes to your overall control during execution.
- Jump directly off your toe pick.
- On the takeoff, keep your head straight and your weight directly over your left leg. This will allow you to achieve maximum height.
- Pay close attention to your line of direction in the air. In order to augment air time, your right leg should thrust behind you but slightly out to the side. When you observe the performance of a Salchow, it may look like the right leg wraps around the left, but in reality your momentum should ensure that the jump travels back behind you. If your right leg comes through behind you at an angle, this will facilitate increased air time.

BEGINNING ONE-FOOT SPIN

Now that you've learned a number of beginning jumps, let's take a break from them and go back to some spinning.

The one-foot spin is known by a variety of names—scratch spin, upright spin, and, our favorite, blur spin. But before you can spin with the speed of an electric mixer, you must first familiarize yourself with the sensation of spinning on one foot.

When you performed the two-foot spin, the lengths of both your blades were in contact with the ice, with one foot moving backward and the other forward. The transition into spinning on one foot requires that you bear weight primarily on the ball of your foot and travel on a back inside edge.

Starting position: Begin by executing a two-foot spin (remember—righties spin counterclockwise, lefties in a clockwise direction). After completing two rotations, maintain an upright body position.

1. Begin picking up your right foot (left foot for lefties). To lift the foot, bend your right knee, pull up on your right thigh, and position the inside of your body gently against your left calf. Make sure to adjust your upper body so that your weight is now balanced over your left leg. Lifting up on the right hip will assist in this weight shift. (Frequently beginners will lean *toward* the leg they're lifting. Avoid this error; it would necessitate putting the foot back down to keep from falling over.)

2. As you pick up your foot, the heel of your left blade should come up slightly off the ice, causing you to spin on the ball of your foot. As this happens, you may feel the bottom of your toe pick coming into contact with the ice. This may feel foreign—but don't fret, and don't fight it.

3. As your momentum fades, you'll need to exit the spin. Place your right foot down flat on the ice. Check your arms out so the left is in front—directly out from, but slightly

A NOTE ON THE ONE-FOOT SPIN

The blade you're standing on should be traveling in small circles on a back inside edge. Ideally, you want the circles to be on top of each other, so that your spin remains in a tight, confined area. If you find yourself wandering across the ice for any great distance—more than, say, 18 inches—you are "traveling." (Patti warns her students that if they travel any farther than 18 inches on a spin, they should think about packing an overnight bag.) Traveling is caused by a lack of balance over the skating leg. To center your spin, make sure to stretch up tall over your skating leg, keeping your head and back upright.

lower than, your left shoulder. Your right arm should be at the same height but out to the side and slightly behind your right hip. Bend both knees. Push back with your left leg, turning the hip and foot out. Fully extend that leg behind you with the heel of the blade aligned behind the heel of your skating foot.

4. Keeping your skating knee bent, your free hip elevated, and your body erect, glide gracefully away from the spin on a back outside edge.

You are now well on your way to becoming a master of basic on-ice jumping and spinning. As you probably know by now, skating looks and sounds a lot easier than it actually is. Hang in there! The best skaters are those who possess a strong sense of determination and a high level of tenacity.

CHAPTER 6

GROUP LESSONS AND PRIVATE INSTRUCTION

The man who is too old to learn was probably always too old to learn.

—Henry S. Haskins

U p until now we have been your personal coaches, providing you with private lessons, bringing you along at your own pace. However, you may find that working on the ice in a group setting with a coach will enhance your learning experience.

Many areas of the country offer group lessons endorsed by either of figure skating's two separate governing bodies in the United States—the Ice Skating Institute (ISI) and the United States Figure Skating Association (USFSA).

ISI

To paraphrase from its *Skaters and Coaches Handbook* (1998 edition): "The ISI has established a group lesson program for those who skate for recreation and enjoyment. It appeals to first-time skaters because it presents movement they can master almost immediately. The ISI has developed a testing system that provides yardsticks for all skaters, from the very beginner (Pre-Alpha) to the most advanced skater (Freestyle 10)."

Most ISI programs are run by rink management. The sessions are generally held once weekly and are six to eight weeks in duration, with a variety of registration times. Registration fees will usually buy you a 30- to 45-minute group lesson, with the same amount of time for practice on your own.

Toward the fourth or fifth week of a learn-to-skate session, registration materials should become available for a continuation of instruction. At this time some sort of evaluation process (on the part of your current instructor) should occur to determine your progress and assist in future class placement. When a new session begins, skaters are frequently shifted into different classes with a subsequent change in instructors.

Although ISI group lessons vary across the country, a group instructional session is always more economical than a private, one-on-one lesson.

While ISI makes its programs and test structures available to member rinks, it does not monitor the day-to-day management of these programs. Always be a good consumer—be assertive in asking questions or voicing your concerns.

To help you determine the class level best suited for your skating ability, the following classifications are used to divide skill levels:

Class Level and Name	Skills to Be Learned
1. Pre-Alpha	Two-foot glide One-foot glide Forward swizzle Backward wiggle Backward swizzle
2. Alpha	Forward stroking Forward crossovers in both directions Snowplow stop
3. Beta	Backward stroking Back crossovers in both directions T-stops with both feet
4. Gamma	Forward outside three turns on both feet Inside mohawks in both directions Hockey stop
5. Delta	Inside three turns in both directions Consecutive forward outside edges Consecutive forward inside edges Shoot-the-duck (duck slide) Forward lunge Bunny hop

Once the skater has mastered skills through the Delta level, the ISI offers a series of Freestyle tests. As such, many ISI learn-to-skate programs offer Freestyle classes.

The elements (many of which we've covered with you) offered in the first three freestyle tests are:

Class Name and Level	Skills to Be Learned
Freestyle 1	Forward inside pivot Two-foot spin Forward arabesque (spiral) Consecutive back outside edges Consecutive back inside edges Half flip Waltz jump

Freestyle 2	Ballet jump
	Half toed walley
	Half lutz
	One-foot spin
	Two different forward arabesques (different feet or different edges)
	Dance step sequence (including mohawks and crossovers)
Freestyle 3	Back outside or inside pivot
	Salchow
	Change-foot spin
	Backward arabesque
	Toe loop
	Dance step sequence (including an outside mohawk)

Upon completion of each of these levels, some programs will award the skater a certificate or badge.

For more information you can contact the ISI at:

Ice Skating Institute
17120 North Dallas Parkway
Suite 140
Dallas, TX 75248-1187
Phone: 972-735-8800
Fax: 972-735-8815
www.skateisi.com

USFSA

The USFSA also offers a learn-to-skate program that it calls Basic Skills, with a current theme of "Skate with U.S." As noted from the *Chevrolet/USFSA Skate with U.S. Coach's Manual for Basic Skills Program* (1998): "The Chevrolet/Skate with U.S. program has a mission to provide a goal-oriented program that encourages ice skating at all levels and to enhance the quality of skating skills at these levels."

To enroll in a USFSA Basic Skills program, you must first join a USFSA club. To locate a club in your area, contact the association's home office in Colorado Springs, Colorado.

United States Figure Skating Association
20 First Street
Colorado Springs, Colorado 80906-3697
Phone: 719-635-5200
Fax: 719-635-9548
www.usfsa.org

You can also call the rinks in your area and ask specifically for the name and number of USFSA clubs that may exist in your town or city.

While an ISI program is usually run by a rink, a USFSA Basic Skills program is run by a club. Like many organizations, the club has a board of directors—usually volunteer parents who have one or more skaters on the ice and involved at some level in a USFSA program.

Most USFSA Basic Skills programs begin in the fall of the year and run once a week through early spring. Generally, there is only one registration session, usually held a week or so before classes begin, and your fee covers all ice-time expenses for the season.

Initially, there may be some shuffling from group to group so that skaters are placed in the class best suited to their needs. Once placement is determined by the instructors, skaters will usually remain in the same class with the same coach for the duration of the season.

A good Basic Skills program should meet the same criteria as outlined for the ISI programs.

The USFSA divides its Basic Skills into the following categories:

Class Name and Level	Skills to Be Learned
Basic 1	Sit on ice and stand up
	March forward across the ice
	Skate forward and glide on two feet
	Glide forward on two feet and dip
	Rocking horse (forward and backward swizzle action)
	Forward two-foot swizzles—six to eight in a row
	Snowplow stop
	Two-foot hop on a spot
	Backward wiggle—six to eight in a row
Basic 2	Forward one-foot glides, right and left
	Continuous forward slalom—six to eight in a row

	Backward two-foot swizzles—six to eight in a row
	Backward two-foot glide
	Continuous backward slalom—four to six in a row
	Two-foot turn (from forward to backward) on a spot
	Moving snowplow stop
Basic 3	Forward stroking showing correct use of blade
	Forward one-foot swizzles (pumping) on a circle, clockwise and counterclockwise
	Backward one-foot swizzles (pumping) on a circle, clockwise and counterclockwise
	Moving forward-to-backward two-foot turns, clockwise and counterclockwise
	Gliding backward on one foot
	Two-foot spin with two revolutions
Basic 4	Forward outside edge on a circle
	Forward inside edge on a circle
	Forward crossovers in both directions
	Forward outside three turns from a T-position—right and left
	Backward snowplow stop, right and left
Basic 5	Backward outside edge on a circle
	Backward inside edge on a circle
	Backward crossovers, clockwise and counterclockwise
	One-foot spin (minimum of three revolutions)
	T-stops, right and left
	Side toe hop—both directions
Basic 6	Forward inside three turns from a T-position—right and left
	Moving backward-to-forward two-foot turns on a circle, clockwise and counterclockwise
	Hockey stop
	Bunny hop
	Forward spiral
	Forward lunge
Basic 7	Forward inside mohawk from a T-position—right and left
	Backward outside to forward outside transition on a circle—right and left

	Ballet jump
	Backward crossovers to a backward outside edge (landing position), clockwise and counterclockwise
	Beginning scratch spin
Basic 8	Moving forward outside three-turn on a circle—right and left
	Moving forward inside three-turn on a circle—right and left
	Standstill waltz jump
	Mazurka
	Combination move: two forward crossovers into a forward inside mohawk, cross behind, step into one backward crossover, step to forward inside edge—repeat three times, clockwise and counterclockwise
	Forward inside pivot, left and right

In our teaching with you we have also covered a number of the skills in the first three USFSA Basic Skills freestyle tests:

Class Name and Level	Skills to Be Learned
Free Skate 1	Advanced forward stroking
	Forward outside and forward inside consecutive edges (four to six edges)
	Scratch spin from backward crossovers (minimum of three revolutions)
	Waltz jump from two or three backward crossovers
	Half flip
	Advanced backward outside three turn, right and left
Free Skate 2	Backward outside and backward inside consecutive edges (four to six edges)
	Waltz jump, side hop, waltz jump sequence
	Forward outside and forward inside spirals, clockwise and counterclockwise, right and left
	Waltz threes, right and left
	Beginning back spin (minimum of one to two revolutions)

	Continuous forward Progressive Chasse sequence, clockwise and counterclockwise
Free Skate 3	Forward and backward crossovers in a figure eight
	Salchow
	Advanced forward consecutive swing rolls (four to six edges)
	Half Lutz jump
	Waltz jump/toe loop jump combination, or Salchow jump/toe loop jump combination
	Backward inside three turn, right and left
	Back spin with free foot in crossed-leg position (minimum of three revolutions)
	Waltz eight

Most coaches have an established sequence for teaching basic skills. While they will cover the elements called for at a certain level, upon evaluation of skaters in their particular group, they may weave in skills from other levels.

YOUR FIRST DAY AT A GROUP LESSON

Prepare yourself. Most likely you'll be walking into mass confusion—adults and kids milling about, five small benches to accommodate 50 large skaters, long lines at the skate rental booth, moms and dads struggling to fit skates onto Junior's wiggling feet.

Rink staff and volunteers may be available to sort things out—maybe. It's best to resign yourself to the fact that this first day may leave you a bit dizzy.

If you've had the good fortune to enroll in a well-organized program, you may find:

- Name tags for each participant
- Some kind of system to direct skaters to their correct group—for instance, color-coded name tags that correspond to colored paper taped to rink Plexiglas
- Instructors and, possibly, assistants on the ice to usher skaters to the correct group

A SPECIAL NOTE FOR PARENTS

If you have a child on the ice and you're her number one fan in the stands, realize that she is subject to a multitude of distractions. As her instructor is attempting to teach a skill, please refrain from banging on the Plexiglas, waving, or blowing kisses as shows of support. There'll be plenty of time for hugs, kisses, and pats on the back when your child exits the ice *after* the session ends.

The actual ice setup for learn-to-skate programs will vary. Some rinks will divide the ice surface in half, with one half further divided into three to five groups for lessons. The remaining half will be left free for open practice. After the designated lesson time ends, skaters will switch halves.

Other programs will divide the ice into width-wide strips to accommodate the number of groups on the ice. (This past year Patti and Nikki taught in one USFSA program that had nine groups.) In this way everyone has the same lesson time and the same practice time.

Remember that your group experience, with lesson and practice, will run one to one and a half hours. Should you start to feel heavy fatigue or exhaustion, take a break, sip some water, and chill out on one of the benches in the hockey box. As we mentioned previously, rink temperatures vary, so bring extra clothing and mittens to layer on if needed. A small box of tissues or a handkerchief is essential, because noses run like crazy at all rinks.

At the end of your first or second session, should you have doubts about proper placement in a group (too high or too low) or seem to have a personality clash with your assigned group's teaching pro, we suggest that you talk with your assigned pro, right away, or with the session supervisor (this person is usually sequestered in the box or the area where the sound system resides). If necessary, you can also speak to the rink's skating director.

Nothing prohibits you from being a member of *both* the ISI and the USFSA. (Both organizations publish an informative, full-

COACHES' CREDENTIALS

Many rinks have updated résumés filed for each of their teaching professionals. Feel free to review these; they will give you some idea of what the coaches achieved and accomplished as *skaters*, including:

- USFSA and ISI tests passed
- Competitions entered (and sometimes the placement)
- Nationally recognized coaches with whom they have trained
- History or details of being a principal or a cast member in a skating show—Ice Capades, Disney on Ice, and so on.

The résumés may also give you some concept of the coaches' experience levels—their number of years teaching, educational background, experience teaching in an other-than-figure-skating setting (preschool, grade school, high school, or the like), pupil accomplishments and achievements, and ice-show productions.

However, solid-gold skating credentials and years of on-ice teaching *do not necessarily* make for a good skating coach. What a résumé will *not* reflect is whether the individual is able to relate and communicate to students (and/or their parents) in a meaningful and productive way.

color magazine containing ads for skates and supplies.) Feel free to sample both learn-to-skate programs. Later, should you choose, you'll be entitled to enter both ISI and USFSA competitions.

We have found that the differences between ISI and USFSA programs at this level are negligible. Basic skills are basic skills no matter which governing organization is involved. The strength or weakness of any program relies primarily on the quality of the coaching.

PICKING A PRO FOR PRIVATE LESSONS

Group lessons are great, but hiring a pro for private lessons will give you one-on-one attention—a distinct advantage that will never be possible in a group setting. In a private lesson a pro can quickly identify a flaw in technique or attend to any question you may have regarding figure skating in general. In essence, you buy the pro's experience and undivided attention for anywhere from fifteen minutes to an hour.

If you have budgetary constraints, be advised that a private lesson will always be more expensive than a group lesson.

Like skaters, pros come in all varieties. Though the choice will always come down to personal preference and instinct, there are a few qualities you should always look for in a pro.

A pro who possesses all the essential qualities will:

- Treat you with respect and dignity.
- Never resort to abuse or condescension.
- Make learning fun and enjoyable.
- Provide a balanced mix of constructive criticism and positive reinforcement.
- Be selectively stern when the occasion demands, but never resort to rude or demeaning language.
- Push to bring out your best without pushing you over the edge.
- Be available to discuss issues and concerns, for a reasonable amount of time, at the end of a skating session.
- Convey sincerity and express belief in you not only as a skater but also as a fellow human being.
- Keep abreast of upcoming events that may be of interest to you—extra ice time, test sessions, competitions, ice shows, skating seminars, and so forth.
- Help you determine, set, and reach your intended goals. However, a consummate pro will also possess enough flexibility to change course should you decide to put your energies elsewhere—into recreational skating rather than competitive skating, for instance, or ice dance versus freestyle, or synchronized skating versus freestyle.
- Keep your enthusiasm high so that you look forward to each and every lesson.
- Adjust teaching strategies to accommodate the special learning styles of each individual student.
- Possess a strong passion for, love of, and dedication to the sport.
- Allow you to leave her tutelage, gracefully and without guilt, should you decide to become a hockey or speed skater—or to leave the sport of ice skating altogether.

IF YOU'RE CONSIDERING A PRO FOR PRIVATE LESSONS

- Observe the pro in action while teaching a private lesson.
- Talk with the pro regarding coaching and learning philosophies.
- Observe the pro off the ice in interactions with skaters, parents, and other staff.
- Here's a tip from Karla, Nikki's younger sister, also a figure skater. The seven-year-old told her parents, "I want Patti 'cos she picks her students up and skates with them. They always seem happy . . . like they're having fun."
- Trust your gut, your instinct, and that little voice inside you.

SKATING SCHOOLS

Although the ISI and USFSA are national organizations, they do not conduct formal licensing of programs or, in some cases, skating schools. An individual needs only a pair of skates to call herself a pro. Skating schools operate under no governing jurisdiction; all they need is access to a sheet of ice.

Again, if you're considering enrolling in a skating school, check the background and credentials of the pros and the organization.

DEDICATED FREESTYLE ICE

Our guess is that, up until now, the majority of your practice has come during public ice sessions. Since you've been acquiring more and more skills, and broadening your knowledge base, now is the time to consider purchasing dedicated freestyle ice.

Clearly, the advantage of public ice is economy. However, as you progress in the sport, here are some of the disadvantages you may encounter:

- You're able to travel in only one direction—clockwise or counterclockwise.
- You're confined to the small coned-in area at the center of the rink often designated for figure skaters during public ice sessions. This limited space prevents you from practicing extensions and jumps.
- Some rinks prohibit the execution of certain figure skating skills during crowded public sessions. (A rink guard may tell you to cease and desist your arabesque.)
- You may encounter heavy traffic (especially on weekends and over school holidays). You may be sharing the ice with skaters at varying skill levels wearing hockey skates, speed skates, and, yes, the dreaded double-runner skates.
- Often unmonitored behavior of out-of-control skaters greatly increases the possibility of collisions.

In most areas there are several options for purchasing dedicated freestyle ice. The rink management may offer sessions that they term "public figure skating." In this situation, although the number of skaters allowed onto the ice may be limited, the ability levels are often mixed. You may find yourself on the ice with a skater performing a triple flip while another clings to the wall for dear life. The only prerequisite for admission to these sessions is that you have *figure* skates on your feet.

Mixed-ability-level sessions can be somewhat dicey. It's difficult to predict where everyone is going. Some beginners feel intimidated sharing the ice with advanced skaters who streak around the rink at the speed of light.

Your other option is to purchase a figure skating session through a club. Frequently this ice can be purchased as a package—one fee buys you a slot of ice time for the entire season. Good figure skating clubs offer separate sessions based on ability level—for ex-

INSIDER'S TIP

Some advanced skaters will intentionally *try* to scare you to the boards, thereby leaving them an open space to launch their triple-whatever jump. Keep moving, but stand your ground. Don't immediately defer to a faster skater. If you were already setting up a move, go for it.

ample, a high-level freestyle session and a low-level freestyle. With this setup both the number of skaters on the ice and their proficiency levels will be regulated by the club. In this way you'll only be on the ice with skaters who are at *approximately* your level. For you, that will probably be a low freestyle session.

Also, club sessions usually have a session supervisor who plays the music and monitors on-ice behavior to ensure everyone's safety. (The supervisor is usually housed in the area where the PA and cassette player reside.) Session supervisors are often volunteer parents or club board members.

To purchase an ice package from a figure skating club, you'll most likely be required to pay an annual membership fee. This fee, like other figure skating fees, ranges from low to high, depending on where you live.

The benefits of joining a club are:

- You'll receive club literature (which sometimes includes skating session times and exclusions, skating coaches' bios and phone numbers, club officers' and board members' names and numbers, and a brief history of the club along with a mission statement).
- You'll receive the magazine published by the club's governing organization (ISI or USFSA).
- You may receive a club newsletter, if the club is inclined to put one out.

If you're a little hesitant about making the commitment to join a particular club, you can test the (frozen) water by "buying on" to a freestyle session. This entails contacting a rink or a club (specifically, the session supervisor) and inquiring whether there is an opening during a particular session. If so, you can reserve yourself a spot. Clubs generally charge a higher fee for nonmembers; some may actually limit the number of buy-ons they'll sell you before you are required to purchase a full club membership.

SUMMER FIGURE SKATING CAMPS AND PROGRAMS

Ice during the summer? Honest! In fact, in some areas there is more figure skating ice available during the summer months than in any other season. A major drawing factor for most summer programs is the opportunity to skate at a regular time on a *daily basis*.

Summer programs fall into two categories—the kind hosted by your local rink and those housed at nationally and/or internationally recognized skating centers. The recognized skating centers usually attract many name pros. (We'll define a *name pro* as "one who has distinguished herself as a competitive skater and/or who has *worked* with one, or a number of National, Olympic, or World champions.")

Let's talk about the differences and similarities between these two categories.

If you enroll in a local summer program you'll have the convenience and economy of commuting from home. If you're a working adult, many programs offer early-morning ice that allows you to skate before you go to work. Your program can last anywhere from a week or two to most if not all of the summer.

Given the intensity level of skating daily, your skill acquisition may accelerate. If seen on a day-to-day basis, your coach (if you've hired one for private lessons) may be more attuned to targeting problem areas in your skating and devising corrective action to remedy them. Additionally, she may introduce you to new elements at a faster rate, knowing you'll have more time to practice them. Lastly, if you're working up a routine for competition, you'll have more time to practice it.

Costwise, remember that ice fees and private pro fees are separate and distinct.

If time and finances permit, you may want to consider summer training at a nationally or internationally recognized skating center. (By midwinter to early spring, these facilities start running advertisements for their programs in the skating magazines. If you're interested, make your inquiries early.)

Consider that before you step onto the ice, you will need to pay for travel (plane, train, bus, or car), lodging, and meals. As with a local program, you'll then need to pay for ice time and private pro fees.

Being in a different area, at a different rink, with different skaters, and—at least temporarily—with a different skating coach can be both exciting and novel. Some skaters want to work with a name pro for the wisdom he may impart, for a new addition to their skating résumé, or simply to come back home and be able to boast, "Yeah, I worked with Richard A. Triplelutzaxel."

Summer camps and programs may also offer off-ice training in the form of dance, plyometrics, fitness classes, trampoline classes, and mental training. (More about off-ice activities in chapter 13.)

Review your skating budget and summer schedule. If you can swing it, cut the check and register for as many weeks as you desire.

The final perk of a summer program is the fact that an ice rink is absolutely the *coolest* place to be during the dog days of summer. So don't be surprised if family and friends are more apt to come see you practice during a sweltering August afternoon versus that frigid February morning.

CHAPTER 7

MENTAL PREPARATION

In order to succeed we must first believe that we can.

—Michael Korda

What the mind can conceive and believe, the mind (and body) can achieve.

—Napoleon Hill

I ce is *slippery*—always has been, always will be. As such, your body has a natural inclination to literally "freeze up" when you venture out onto its surface. Unfortunately, the more tense and stiff you are, the more difficult it is to glide gracefully and elegantly across the ice.

Mental preparation before you skate, along with experience on the ice, will help you relax and skate a session that is both pleasurable and productive.

There are three mental training exercises that we recommend you perform before every skate session, with or without your coach. They are:

- Visualization
- Self-talk
- Relaxation

Think of visualization and self-talk as happening in your head, and relaxation as occurring in your body. Also, regard all three as interrelated, all part of one continuous connection between mind and body.

For example, if you tell yourself (self-talk) that an upcoming test at school or a pending project at work is going to have a disastrous outcome, notice the feeling you generate in your body. You might label it *tense, uncomfortable, nervous, jittery.* In any event, the sensation, the feeling in your body—whether it be in your stomach, chest, neck, or shoulders—is the *opposite* of relaxation.

Now, if you were to construct a picture inside your head (visualization) of yourself lying on a beach, or lazily swinging in a hammock on a warm summer afternoon, or floating on an air mattress in a backyard swimming pool, your corresponding body sensation would most likely be labeled *relaxation.* Your breathing would be slow and even, your neck, chest, and shoulders free of stress, and there would be a distinct *lack* of tension in the pit of your stomach. This is because there is a connection between the body and mind. Think of it this way: Around noontime, the following process occurs for each and every one of us. The body (specifically the stomach) notices that it hasn't been fed in a while. It sends a signal, an awareness, to the brain. There, a little voice inside your head whispers, "Burger and fries," and a little picture of a burger and fries suddenly appears inside your mind. The next thing you know you're pulling up to the drive-through window.

Because this process is looped and the three elements (visualization, self-talk, body sensations) are interrelated, the experience can also happen first on an inner audio or an inner visual level.

For example, suppose you're really engrossed in some form of work or play, and the signal from your stomach isn't noticed by the brain. After a while you glance up at your wall clock, which reads 12:30 P.M.

"Oh, lunchtime!" a reminder voice speaks within your mind.

Within nanoseconds you visualize a tuna melt with a side order of slaw. Your mouth waters and your stomach begins to growl hungrily. Your work or play is set aside and you shuffle off to the restaurant.

Mind and body—connected.

In all probability, before you step onto the ice—whether you're in the car, in the warming room, or walking (guards on!) across the rubber mats on your way to the entrance of the rink—you're making an inner image, a mental movie of yourself falling on the ice.

Your body tenses, anticipating the fall. Or you find your inner dialogue (sometimes even spoken out loud) repeating phrases like, "Oh God, I know I'm gonna lose an edge and fall!" Or, "What if I take another skater down with me?" Or, "Those back crossovers are going to kill me!" Here again, your body, trouper that it is, braces itself for the upcoming catastrophe.

For a time, when he had fantasies of being the next Greg LeMond, Bernie spent his summers bike racing. He found, however, that he always hit the brakes when diving into a tight corner. As he slowed, other racers passed him, leaving him at the back of the pack.

When he analyzed what he was doing mentally, he realized that he was *visualizing* a crash. Hence, seized with fear, his body responded by having his fingers squeeze down hard on the brake levers. Ironically, he made himself *more likely* to fall, because these panic stops often caused the bike to shudder and skid.

Hoping to remedy the situation, Bernie sought out the best bike racer in the area and asked him, "What do you think about when you go into a corner?"

The guy looked him straight in the eye, smiled, and replied, "Keeping the bike upright."

Simple as that.

Always conjure up a mental success video, or speak to yourself in such a way that you hear about a positive outcome rather than a negative.

Now let's make this into a practical plan for you.

VISUALIZATION EXERCISES

Before you enter the rink, take just a few minutes in a quiet place—at home or in your parked car—to mentally prepare yourself for a session of skating.

First, close your eyes and visualize yourself skating well—staying upright, stroking smooth and easy, maintaining a steady flow, and completing your jumps and spins. The images may be bright and rich with color or simply black and white. Either way is acceptable for our purposes.

There are actually two ways to visualize. If you see yourself skating as if you were watching it on TV or a movie screen, this is called *dissociated visualization*. If, when you visualize, it feels like you're actually there on the rink, looking out with your own two eyes, seeing the other skaters, the ice, the boots on your feet, it's known as *associated visualization.*

Whether you visualize in an associated or dissociated fashion, it's important to make the experience as multisensational as possible. That is to say, bring into the picture as many of your senses as you can. *Hear* the voices of the other skaters and the sound of your blades cutting into the ice. *Smell* the crispness of the air. *Feel* the cold breeze against your face, your feet firmly in your boots, your balance and your edges gripping solidly as you push and glide across the rink.

Although some mental trainers and sports psychologists argue that associated visualization is a more realistic simulation of the event, whatever appears in your mind when you run the movie is just fine. Some athletes find that while visualizing, they automatically alternate back and forth between associated and dissociated visualization.

Your entire visualization session should last but a few minutes. You can visualize individual elements, an entire program, or both. When you're done, simply allow the image to fade or slip from your mind and slowly open your eyes.

SELF-STATEMENT EXERCISES

Now repeat to yourself (either inside your head or out loud) three positive self-statements about you and your skating. You can write them down on a 3- by 5-inch index card or invent different sentences or phrases for each new session. Whatever you say to yourself, it should always incorporate elements of:

- Fun
- Positive expectancy
- Belief in self

Although the number of self-statements you can write is limitless, and should be unique to you, here are three examples:

- I love to skate.
- I'm really looking forward to this session.
- I'm right where I'm supposed to be.

BODY RELAXATION EXERCISE

Let's work on the last piece of your mental training—body relaxation. Now, we don't want you walking into the rink as limp as a rag doll, so the procedure will be brief. Its purpose is to rid yourself of any excess body tension, any stress, that would detract from a good skating session.

The method is as follows:

Take a full, deep breath in, hold it, and then exhale slowly, letting all the air out. Your head should lower a bit and your shoulders drop. Now let your breathing return to its normal cadence and rhythm. Focus on the sound of your breathing and the rise and fall of your chest for a few moments. Then start to imagine that with your next inhalation, you're bringing into your body:

1. Relaxation

And with the next inhalation, you're pulling in:

2. Inner peace

And with the next:

3. Calm

And the next:

4. Confidence

Now begin to imagine that with your next *exhalation* of breath, along with the used air, the spent gases, you're breathing out:

1. Any remaining stress or tension

And with the next exhalation, you're breathing out:

2. Any worrisome thoughts or distractions

And with the next:

3. Any negativity

And the next:

4. Any self-doubt

When you're finished with this cycle of two "fours" (four inhalations, four exhalations), open your eyes and welcome yourself back into the here and now.

Your entire experience of mental preparation—visualization, self-talk, and relaxation—should take about 5 or 10 minutes.

Don't worry if someone sees you with your eyes closed and chattering to yourself. Most people think figure skaters are a little wacky anyway.

This last point is a good segue into discussing a fear that many beginning skaters tend to grapple with: "What will people think of me?"

In our experience, teens and adults seem to be the most vulnerable to this particular anxiety; little kids tend not to worry. They're out there slipping, sliding, giggling, and falling in all sorts of bizarre positions, having a grand old time. They couldn't care less about what others might think about their performance.

But by early adolescence self-consciousness—often excessive, sometimes obsessive—begins to creep in. Specifically, figure skaters often fear:

- Embarrassing themselves
- Negative evaluation—by coaches, other skaters, and/or spectators

Learning to skate is an awkward, often ungraceful process. You're attempting not only to hold your balance on a thin 2-inch-high piece of metal that rides up the center of your boot, but also to navigate your way across a surface that's as slick as, well, ice! And it's *supposed* to be difficult; otherwise, anyone who ever laced up a boot would quickly join the ranks of the millionaire superstars (and yes, they too still fall).

If you accept the following two principles, your embarrassment should ease, if not evaporate altogether:

- Awkwardness is present with any new sport-skill acquisition, and never more so than with the elements found in figure skating. Skating is a sport of patience and perseverance. Grace and flow come with time.
- Falling is an integral part of skating, not the enemy. You fall, you get up, and start skating again. It's a lot like life in general.

The only times you should ever feel embarrassed are:

- You show up for an early-morning session still dressed in your pajamas.
- You exit the bathroom with a 12-inch strip of toilet paper flapping merrily behind you, stuck tight to the ridges of one of your blade guards.

Now let's tackle any concerns you might have about negative evaluation by others at the rink.

If you get a dirty look or a rude comment from another skater, brush it off; it will usually come from one of the prima donnas who are omnipresent at any rink. These darlings are inadequate individuals who channel their energy into scapegoating others rather than focusing on self-improvement. Don't let them spoil your precious moments of enjoyment.

Similarly, should you glance into the stands and catch what appears to be a look of disdain from a spectator, remember—*you're* the one who's mustered the guts to actually get out there and learn a new skill. The spectator is simply that: one who watches life pass by from the sidelines, never involved, never facing the fear that prevents a rich, *active* involvement in life.

One last tip.

As you make your way to the entrance of the rink, hold your head high, put a slight smile on your lips, and walk with a confident stride. Your body posture will send one last message to your brain:

"I can do this!"

CHAPTER 8

ICE ETIQUETTE

Hell is other people.

—No Exit, Jean-Paul Sartre

Close your eyes and imagine yourself looking out onto a freshly Zambonied sheet of ice—no scratches, no ruts, no . . . people. See how the ice sparkles, glistens, beckons you onto its surface.

Now open your eyes and come back to reality. Unless you're testing or it's your turn to take to the ice for your solo freestyle or dance competition, this visual will forever remain a fantasy. The fact is, 99 percent of the time that you're skating you'll have to contend with . . .

Other people.

In some ways this seems unfair, because skating is such a solitary activity. Still, in this chapter we'll help you to maximize your skating enjoyment while minimizing the frustration that comes from skating with the masses.

In a perfect world skaters and coaches would all act in a courteous and respectful manner while occupying the ice with you. Like our world, however, the ice rink will always remain imperfect. Although you might be able to influence the behavior of others, you'll never be able to control it. You can control your *own* actions on the ice, though. We've outlined some appropriate ice behaviors for you with the wish that perhaps others might learn from your example.

REGARDING YOUR OWN ON-ICE BEHAVIOR

- Coming away from the wall is a lot like crossing the street—always look both ways before making your move.
- When skating backward, it is *your* responsibility to look behind and watch for others.
- If you need to tighten your laces or take a socialization break with friends or acquaintances, move into one of the hockey boxes so as not to impede the progress of other skaters.
- Be careful when performing any move that involves an outstretched blade, such as a spiral.
- At no time should you be standing stationary anywhere on the ice for an extended period of time. Making like a statue makes it difficult for others to maneuver around you. (Also, remember the old adage: A moving target is harder to hit.)
- If you fall, get up as quickly as possible.
- If you come upon a downed skater who appears to be injured, ask if she needs help. Don't move or attempt to pull the skater to a standing position. Summon the session supervisor or a rink guard—either of whom should be trained in first-aid procedures.
- If possible, avoid skating between a coach and her skater while a lesson is in progress.
- Perform your spins in the middle of the rink. Practicing spinning near the wall can present a safety hazard to yourself and others should your spin travel smack dab into the dasher.

REGARDING THE BEHAVIORS OF OTHERS

Unfortunately, you may be witness to a plethora of inappropriate behaviors from both skaters and coaches at the rink. So that they come as no surprise to you, we list a few examples:

- Coaches berating their students in a loud and disruptive manner.
- Prima donnas throwing tantrums should they perceive that someone is in their way. Likewise, an ice diva is prone to a hissy fit should she pop a jump (bail out in midair) or blow a spin.
- Overinvolved but unqualified (nonqualified?) parents coaching from the sidelines. (We have seen parents shouting from the bleachers, pacing the hockey boxes, and, in one instance, actually mounting the Plexiglas in order to bark out a command!)
- Coaches and skaters mocking other skaters by word or action or reveling at the sight of a skater's fall.
- Coaches standing in the middle of the rink, intentionally getting in the way or blocking the path of another coach's skater.
- Coaches actively soliciting skaters and parents who are already committed to the services of another coach.
- Skaters who appear unaware of the presence of others—for instance, by plowing through a group with blatant disregard for safety.
- Skaters who, when their program music is being played over the PA, expect others to cower and clutch at the boards when they pass.

If a coach should ask you to stop spinning or jumping while her skater is practicing a program, you are *not* required to comply with her request.

Most rinks have their fair share of prima donnas and ice divas. Due to their high level of proficiency, they often operate as though they are rulers of the ice kingdom.

Remember, everyone has paid the same amount for ice time, and so everyone is entitled to equal ice privileges. Courtesy should be reciprocal. If respect is not coming your way, let it go, move on, and don't allow yourself to fall victim to intimidation.

When dealing with others at the rink, be respectful, be assertive, and remember that regardless of ability level *all* skaters have an equal share of that ice. When it comes to safety, practice the rink equivalent of driving defensively.

Shoot for reciprocal courtesy. The Golden Rule nails it: Do unto others as you'd have them do unto you.

CHAPTER 9

ADDITIONAL SKATING DISCIPLINES

What we love to do we find time to do.

—John Lancaster Spalding

By now, we assume, you've mastered many of your basic skills—through us, or a group session, or private lessons with a pro, or a combination of all three. You've also been introduced to freestyle, a solo discipline of figure skating. So let's explore some other forms of the sport in which you may cultivate an interest.

ICE DANCE

Ice dance is a combination of intricate steps and edges performed in specific patterns to different rhythms. In essence, it is ballroom dancing on ice, and can be performed solo or with a partner. Ice dance runs the gamut of moods, from the staid stateliness of a waltz to the high sensuousness of a tango.

Ice dance may appeal to you if you've discovered that you're not all that enamored with jumping and spinning but still want to express yourself in a form that lends itself to dramatic interpretation.

The USFSA and the International Skating Union (ISU) have developed a series of more than 30 dances termed compulsory dances. Included are waltzes, tangos, foxtrots, cha-chas, and a couple of polkas. In compulsory dances, edges, crossovers, and turns are combined in a specific order that repeats itself on the ice.

Although it's enjoyable to dance solo, you can double your fun with a partner. And when skating with a partner, each dance has its own prescribed handhold.

If skated with a partner, the Dutch Waltz (for example) uses what's called the kilian position. The female is on the male's right, both partners facing straight ahead. The female's left arm is in front of the male's chest, her hand resting on top of his as he holds on to her thumb. The male's left arm is parallel to the ice, slightly lower than shoulder height, with the elbow bent.

The male's right arm is behind the female's back. She rests her thumb in the web between his thumb and forefinger, and he holds her hand onto her hipbone.

Kilian position

One of the main attractions of any of the compulsory dances is being able to skate it to specific music. Each of the dances has its own identifying rhythm. Although there are a number of different waltzes, each one has a specific number of beats per minute.

Most figure skating clubs and some rinks own audiocassettes of *all* dance music. Barring specific restrictions, they will certainly play a dance upon request while you're on freestyle ice. Due to demand and popularity, some clubs offer dedicated dance sessions, where only dance may be practiced.

If dance really hooks you, you'll probably want to purchase your own set of tapes so that, along with ice sessions, you can practice to your heart's content across your living room carpet. To locate the tapes, you can:

- Scan a copy of the USFSA magazine for retailers that market the tapes through mail order.
- Contact the USFSA national headquarters in Colorado Springs, Colorado.

Also, annually the USFSA publishes a rulebook containing diagrams and descriptions of all the compulsory dances, additional information about each dance, and definitions of ice dance terminology. Contact the USFSA for price and purchase procedure.

Other Aspects of Ice Dance

Should you become a fan of watching competitive ice dance on TV, you'll soon discover that compulsory dances are worth 20 percent of the final score. The remaining 80 percent comes from two additional forms of ice dance: the "original dance" and the "free dance."

Each year the ISU selects a dance tempo to be used for the original dance—tango, rock and roll, polka, blues, waltz, or the like. The dance teams (duos) then must choreograph their own particular interpretation of that mandated selection. The original dance counts for 30 percent of the overall score.

The free dance, valued at a whopping 50 percent, has the fewest number of restrictions in terms of what the dance teams can actually put onto the ice. This facet of ice dance resembles *pair skating* (see section on next page) in that you'll see a number of lifts.

The male, for instance, might hoist his partner into the air, but never with his hands above his shoulders. You might also see a series of small jumps and abbreviated spins, but never triple or quadruple jumps or spins with blinding multirevolutions.

Primarily the dance duo skates together, rarely separating for longer than 10 seconds. Skaters can choose their own music for the free dance, but selections must abide by ISU guidelines.

Ice dance may constitute the most controversial form of figure skating: There seems to be a somewhat confusing, wide-open approach to interpretation of rules. Due to this, the last several Winter Olympic Games saw much heated discussion about the fairness and objectivity of the judging. Rule revisions are ongoing, to hopefully remedy this situation.

PAIR SKATING

Whether you're watching an event on TV or from the audience of a millionaire-superstar live show, you may notice that pair skating shares common ground with ice dance. Both disciplines require one male and one female skater to work together as a team. As long and as hard as you may channel-surf, you'll never see a telecast of a solo ice dancer.

Pairs part company with dance, however, in that it features many of the jumps and spins seen in freestyle, along with some outrageous lifts, twists, and throws. You can be an ice dancer without a partner, taking tests, receiving badges, even competing solo. Not so with pairs.

Of all the figure skating disciplines, we regard pair skating as the most dangerous, involving the most risk factors—the height of the lifts, the velocity and difficulty of the throw jumps, and the fact that you're skating in very close proximity to your partner.

Because statistically there are more females in the sport of figure skating, finding a male partner is sometimes the first challenge. (This also holds true for ice dance.)

Once you've built yourself a pretty solid repertoire of freestyle skills, you may want to try skating pairs. The second hurdle (after locating a partner and a good coach) is to learn to skate in unison. You'll also need a great deal of upper-body strength, so break out the weight bench or seek out the services of a personal trainer who can target the specific muscle groups you'll need to develop.

Your coach, in varying sequences (depending on his philosophy and preference), would probably work with you on:

- **Side-by-side jumps:** Both skaters perform the same jump, in unison, in close proximity to each other.
- **Side-by-side solo spins:** The pair, in unison, execute the same spin, completing the same number of revolutions. The challenge here is that the spins need to be synchronized, with each skater exiting the spin at the same time.
- **Pair spins:** The partners are connected by holding each other (hooking their legs together, for instance) and spin together with the goal of appearing to be one unit.
- **Throw jumps:** The female jumps, with an assist from the male to make her jump higher, longer, and more spectacular. When all goes well, the flier lands gracefully gliding backward on one foot.
- **Lifts:** Traditionally, the male lifts the female, although there is no rule against reversing the roles. A move is considered a lift when at least one of the lifter's hands is above shoulder height. Lifts vary. One of the most dramatic is the split twist lift, in which the female is tossed into the air, spins, and is caught by her partner.
- **Death spirals:** While performing a back pivot, the male supports the female by holding on to one of her hands. The female circles the male, supporting herself on a very deep one-foot edge with her head dropped back, and her back arched and parallel to the ice. In the death spiral the female can be traveling forward or backward on an inside or an outside edge. Yet another dangerous but absolutely thrilling move to watch.

SYNCHRONIZED TEAM SKATING

Synchronized team skating, formerly known as *precision team skating,* has been gaining in popularity in both USFSA and ISI clubs in recent years. In a sport dominated by solo and duo skating, being part of a team can give you a sense of camaraderie and allow you to share an exciting and rewarding experience with others.

The objective in synchronized skating is for a group of skaters to work as a team, skating in unison to music as one unit. At its best, a synchronized team functions like a well-oiled machine, with each skater contributing an integral part to the overall whole.

Think of the Rockettes, only on ice.

When elite teams perform, the transitions between formations appear to be seamless; one moment they are hooked at their shoulders, skating forward in razor-sharp lines, and then in the blink of an eye they're holding hands, skating backward in a circle. Along with specific synchronized skating formations, teams also use many moves in their choreography with which you are already familiar—spirals, mohawks, three turns, and lunges. However, as with ice dance, skaters don't perform high-level jumps or spins, so if you've discovered that you're not completely enamored with spending time airborne or whirling like a top, synchronized team skating may hold more appeal for you than freestyle. Also, many skaters who would feel skittish competing solo find their comfort levels as members of a group.

A team consists of 8 to 32 skaters, depending on its affiliation—USFSA or ISI. Additionally, males and females may skate on the same team.

Many teams skate to music that centers on a theme. Broadway shows and movie scores are quite popular. Teams often wear costumes that reflect their chosen theme music. For example, if a team is skating to various pieces of music from the Walt Disney movie *Aladdin,* skaters might wear harem pants, vests, and gold hair scrunchies that resemble, or in some way approximate, costuming from the film. A team skating to various selections of western music might wear outfits with a cowboy or cowgirl flair.

The costs of becoming a member of a synchronized skating team vary greatly. Some teams choose to remain low-key, performing in local exhibitions and local competitions only. They might practice just once or twice a week and be costumed in relatively sim-

Synchronized team in action

ple outfits. If you want to mix and match individual freestyle skating with membership in this type of team, then, you'll experience few conflicts—if any.

Other teams go all out, with an emphasis on competition, hoping to place well on a regional, national, and perhaps international level. Travel to various competitive events may take them across the country or overseas. Such teams usually practice several times a week; in addition to their elaborate costumes, team members may arrive at the rink with matching warm-up suits, skate bags, and so on. Obviously, as ice-time, travel, and costume expenses increase, so do each skater's expenditures. Your decision about what type of synchronized team to join hinges on your personal preferences, your budget, and what your local clubs are currently offering.

If we've sparked a bit of interest in synchronized team skating, why not check it out? You can join a team that's already up and running or look for a fledgling team where all of you will be starting from ground zero. If there are no existing or soon-to-start teams in your city or town, pitch the idea to a club official or a coach. Because volunteers perform so much of the work in skating clubs (supervising sessions, writing newsletters, organizing a year's worth of ice time), you may be asked to spearhead a movement to solicit synchronized team members.

COMPULSORY FIGURES

Hey, this is supposed to be a book about *figure* skating, and we've yet to talk about those very precise elements called figures. What's the story?

When is the last time you went to a live skating event and watched a performer—with *no* accompanying music—execute tracings in the form of a figure eight on a small rectangle of ice called a patch? This may give you a clue as to why compulsory figures are coming so late in the text.

Before fans and figure skaters alike became enamored with freestyle and perhaps more than a little obsessed with multirevolution jumps, figure skating was primarily about exactly what the name implies—skating figures.

Compulsory or "school" figures are a series of exercises practiced and performed on a designated rectangle of ice called a patch. There are 71 different variations of the compulsory figure, all based on the configuration of the figure eight. The figure eight, however, is only the beginning of what becomes an extremely complex series of turns, edges, changes, and loops. Ask any skater who's ever skated "patch," and she will tell you how demanding and complicated the figures become.

The USFSA has divided the 71 figures into a series of nine different tests of increasing difficulty. The first is called the Preliminary Figure Test; the following are assigned the titles of First through Eighth.

The concept of compulsory figures originated in England in the late 1600s and early 1700s. Back then, skaters had to demonstrate the ability to skate a circle on each foot before they could be considered for membership in a skating club. This requirement is considered the root of what eventually evolved into compulsory figures.

From there, the English continued to develop more concepts, invent new turns, and expand on the basic figure eight. In 1892 the International Skating Union (ISU) was created. The English skating pioneers submitted a list of 41 different school figures. Eventually— after innovations and additions from Germany and Austria—this list grew to its current number.

Compulsory figures lay the foundation for all the disciplines of figure skating. Contained within the 71 different school figures are all the edges, changes of edge, changes of direction, and turns necessary to master every freestyle and ice dance maneuver. Indeed, compulsory figures were expressly developed to provide the best technical foundation on which a skater could progress.

Compulsory figures develop:

- Control
- Mastery of outside and inside edges, both forward and backward
- Superior and consistent technique
- Self-discipline
- Powers of concentration
- Correct posture, style, form, and flow
- The ability to move slowly and change direction with no disruption of balance or flow
- Flowing transitions from skate to skate, and from edge to edge
- Correct body lines

- Precision and accuracy of movement
- Proper use of blades
- Strong weight-shifting ability

When practicing school figures, skaters can use an instrument called a scribe. Think of a very large compass (the type used to draw a circle, not find your way out of the woods), set to the height dimensions of the skater that is used to "inscribe" a circle onto the ice. The drawing point of a scribe is aluminum.

In competition or test situations, however, the expectation is that the skater can independently form correctly sized and symmetrical circles without the aid of a mechanical device.

After pushing off onto a figure eight, a skater's blade leaves a mark on the ice called a tracing or print. Examination of this tracing determines:

- Whether the size and shape of the circle is accurate
- If the skater is on the correct part of the blade
- Whether the correct edge is achieved and maintained
- If the skater has wobbled or dragged the free foot

For the skater, the judging of the compulsory figures (whether in a test or a competition) can be an unnerving experience. During freestyle, judges sit to the side of the rink, in hockey boxes, or elevated in a section of the stands. For figures, judges actually stand on the ice with the skaters.

Once the skater completes three repetitions of the figure being judged, she retreats to the side of the rink. The judges converge on the just-completed tracing. They pace off the circles, checking the accuracy of the long and short axes as well as the turn placement. Then some judges actually get down on their hands and knees to study the print.

A combination of factors have contributed to the demise of school figures as an integral part of training for figure skaters.

From the first World Championship in 1896 until the World and Olympic championships of 1972, compulsory figures counted for *two thirds* of the skating competitor's final score. The catalyst for change came in the form of Beatrix Schuba, a competitive skater from Austria.

In the 1972 Olympics Beatrix was so far ahead of her fellow competitors after the completion of the compulsory figures that es-

sentially all she needed to do for the four-minute freestyle component of the competition was stroke around the rink—and she'd win
the gold! And although she did do more than simple stroking, many
felt that her performance was less than inspirational. ISU officials
were dismayed and inundated with demands for change.

After 1972, figures were reduced to only 50 percent of the final
score, then 30 percent, and finally dropped completely from *international* competition after the 1990 competitive season.

While the ISU dealt with the new configurations of competitions
at the national and international levels, skaters, coaches, parents, and
television networks contributed their opinions about school figures.

Skaters and coaches complained about the hours of tedious
practice time needed to master figures at any level. Parents disliked
the expense of purchasing patch sessions and additional lesson time.
Network TV deemed the slow tempo, lack of music, and lack of excitement in compulsory figures unattractive to the general viewing
public. Many involved in the sport felt that the hours spent perfecting compulsory figures would be better spent perfecting advanced
jump and spin techniques.

The result of all this cumulative negative feedback and input was
the complete elimination of figures at *all levels* of national and international competition at the close of the 1999 competitive season.

Although compulsory figures are still part of the testing program offered through the USFSA, skating clubs and rink management no longer find it financially feasible to offer a significant
amount of patch time. As a beginning skater, then, this may be a
component of the sport that you will never experience.

But the next time you see an old patch scribe at a garage sale,
lying next to the eight-track tape player, the manual typewriter, and
a stack of LP record albums, pick it up, hold it in your hands, and
try to imagine the skater who spent hours on the ice under specifically dimmed patch lights, endlessly tracing and retracing patterns
on that figure eight.

MOVES IN THE FIELD

Designed primarily to replace compulsory figures, Moves in the
Field consist of a series of patterns skated around the rink that incorporate the precision edges and turns that were seen in figures,

along with the power and strength necessary for freestyle. They were developed after the demise of figures, when the USFSA wanted a program to teach the same skills imparted by compulsory figures, but in a less restrictive and time-consuming manner.

"Moves," as they're called, develop power, edge quality and control, quickness, extension, precision, good posture, footwork control, and overall flow. Some of the skills necessary to master the beginning Moves test are already in your repertoire—by us or through the ISI or USFSA.

Moves are broken down into eight different skill levels that correspond to the USFSA's freestyle levels. The first few tests are relatively easy; the first test, titled Pre-Preliminary Moves in the Field, was devised to encourage beginners to perfect skating basics. Soon, though, the tests become more difficult and complex.

Each level of Moves in the Field includes three to six different patterns that you must complete, with each pattern focusing on specific types of skills. Usually amateur judges are brought to the rink for scheduled test sessions on a monthly or semimonthly basis; skaters are judged individually.

In the learn-to-skate programs, skills tests are administered by skating coaches. In the first or Pre-Preliminary Moves test you will be performing in front of judges who have been trained and endorsed by USFSA. The test may be judged by either one or three judges. If you see more than three judges, the others are "trial judges." These judges aren't waiting to convict and sentence you should you skate poorly; they're simply USFSA judges-in-training.

When Moves tests are given, the judges generally stand on the ice or are sequestered in hockey boxes. And when those judges are watching, here's what they'll see in that Pre-Preliminary test.

Forward Perimeter Stroking

From a T-position in one corner of the rink, you execute four to eight strokes down the length of the rink. When you approach the end of the rink, you perform crossovers around the end, then four to eight strokes down the other side of the rink, followed by more crossovers that return you to your original starting position. The stroking must be performed in both counterclockwise and clockwise directions. The primary focus is on power, the secondary on extension.

Basic Consecutive Edges

Using a red or blue hockey line as an axis, begin at one wall and perform four to six forward outside edges *across* the rink. Upon reaching the other side, turn around and execute four to six forward inside edges *back* to the other side. At this point you perform four to six back outside edges across the rink, turn around, and execute the same number of back inside edges on the return trip. The primary focus is on edge quality.

Waltz Eight

This maneuver is performed in two circles in a figure-eight pattern. The circles should be relatively large—approximately four to five times your own height. Each circle is skated in a waltz rhythm and counted out in three sets of six beats. Begin in the middle of the figure-eight pattern in a T-position with your right foot leading. Your left arm is out in front, its heel aligned with your belly button. Your right arm is out to the side, stretched slightly back.

For the first count of six, stroke onto a right forward outside edge, then draw your free-foot toe *in behind* your skating heel while maintaining a slightly flexed skating knee. Begin counting on the push; when you reach the fourth beat perform a right outside three turn. Beats five and six should be on a controlled back inside glide in a checked position, with your head looking behind and over your left shoulder.

For the beginning of the next six beats, maintain head and arm position—your right arm in front, your left in back and aligned with your left bun cheek. Then perform a back outside stroke, pushing with your right foot and stepping onto a left back outside edge. These six beats are essentially a back outside edge. After the push, pick up your right foot in front, with the heel aligned in front of your left toes. Then bend your free leg back so that its toe is directly behind your skating-foot heel and your legs are pressed together. Your arms are now dropped to your sides, and the position reversed. Turn your head to the right and back so that you are now looking at the imaginary circle 2 or 3 feet behind you. At this point you should be approximately two thirds of the way around the circle.

For the last six beats, hold your arms still and step forward onto a right outside edge, with your right arm leading and your left arm directly behind you. Your free (left) leg should be bent at the knee, with its toe drawn in behind your skating-foot heel. Then slowly sneak your free foot forward so that as the center (the meeting place between the two circles) is approached, your free foot is directly in front of your skating foot. At the center, push off onto a left forward outside edge and repeat the entire process in the other direction.

The full figure-eight pattern must be performed twice.

Forward Right- and Left-Foot Spirals

This move may be performed either across the width or down the length of the rink. Starting with two or three introductory strokes, execute a forward spiral on one leg in either a straight line or a slight curve. Upon reaching the midline, change feet and perform a spiral on your other leg. The spiral should be held for about four seconds and the free leg elevated to hip level or higher. The emphasis in this Move is on extension.

At any point during the test a judge may ask you to repeat an element. Called a reskate, this can occur only once during a test. Reskates are requested if the judge senses that you can perform the element at a higher level of quality.

Future Moves tests are graded with a numerical score, while the Pre-Preliminary uses only "pass" or "retry." If a grade of retry is given, you must wait 27 days before attempting the test again.

Frequently, judges write comments (positive and negative) on the test sheets. Negative comments should be viewed as constructive criticism. They can steer you (and your coach, if you've retained one) toward improvements in upcoming lessons.

Once you've reviewed the test sheet, you must return it to the club official who is responsible for submitting such information to USFSA national headquarters.

The names of the next seven levels of Moves tests correspond with the names of the USFSA Freestyle categories—Preliminary, Pre-Juvenile, Juvenile, Intermediate, Novice, Junior, Senior—and must be passed before you'll be allowed to take the Freestyle test. For example, you must pass the Preliminary Moves test before you can test

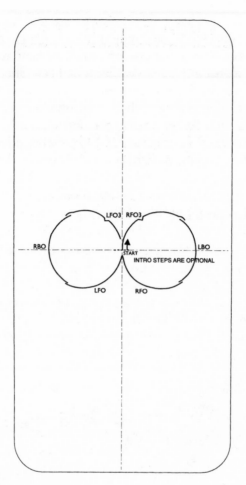

Waltz eight pattern (courtesy USFSA)

Preliminary Freestyle. You may, however, take all the Moves tests without ever attempting any of the Freestyle tests.

Additional information, and descriptions of skills required at each level of Moves in the Field, can be found in the official USFSA rulebook.

CHAPTER 10

TESTING

Anything you're good at contributes to happiness.

—Bertrand Russell

For some skaters, the sense of accomplishment experienced after mastering a skill or a set of elements is enough. Others may want to have their figure skating moves and elements evaluated by those in a position to judge form and quality.

Hence, the figure skating test.

ISI TESTING

ISI testing is usually done by an on-staff professional when he deems that you are ready to take the test.

ISI testing is free unless you'd like a badge. Should you request one, you will be charged a nominal fee for an embroidered keepsake of your accomplishment.

In ISI you can test:

- Dance
- Freestyle

- Pairs
- Couples
- Figures

Note that pairs is always made up of one male and one female. Couples may be same sex.

In order for your test to be registered with the ISI national headquarters, you must first be a member of the ISI. Membership also makes you eligible to compete in any ISI competition. Many ISI learn-to-skate programs also perform informal testing to determine correct placement within lesson groups. These tests tend not to be registered with the national office.

In ISI testing for freestyle, couples, and pairs, you're asked to execute each element at your determined level. You may have a "retry" of each element once—if you or the judge so desires.

Once you've demonstrated the required elements (in freestyle, couples, or pairs) individually, the elements then must be incorporated into a routine set to music. The length of the program is set by the ISI.

You can test anytime you (or your coach) feel a sense of readiness. You can retest as frequently as you wish if you don't pass on your first attempt.

For the higher-level tests in freestyle and dance, a videotape of the entire testing procedure must be created and sent to the ISI national office. The video must be *continuous* (the camera running nonstop from beginning to end) with absolutely no edits. Each solo element must be attempted twice, followed by a performance of the program to music. Once completed, along with mailing the tape you must include a $25 fee.

USFSA TESTING

Testing with the USFSA is a bit more involved and more complex than ISI testing. To begin with, USFSA test sessions must be organized and sanctioned by the board of directors from one of your local USFSA clubs. USFSA tests can only be judged by amateurs in the skating community who have been trained and appointed by the USFSA.

To receive a judging appointment, an individual endures a rigorous training period in which she apprentices with established judges and performs a substantial number of hours of trial judging—viewing and judging skating tests while sitting alongside established judges. At the end of the test, the judge-in-training compares and discusses her results with the mentor judges.

There are many different levels of judges, starting with those who are qualified to judge only beginning-level skaters and ranging right on up through those who can judge national and international events. Each time a judge wants to advance and add to her judging credentials, she must undergo more training.

Although each individual USFSA club picks up the tab—meals, lodging, transportation—when bringing judges on-site for a test session, judges *are not* and *cannot be* paid for their services. Hence, judging is not a paying profession but more an active avocation, a labor of love for the sport. Judges find part- or full-time employment in other fields.

Judges come from various backgrounds. Some are former skaters, some have children who are (or were) skaters, and some have progressed from being spectators to a much more active involvement in the sport that they have grown to love.

Club Preparation for a USFSA Test Session

Each USFSA club designates a test chairperson who is responsible for organizing the test session. (The job can be quite demanding . . . and all on a volunteer basis.) Among other responsibilities, this designee should:

- Meet with the club skating coaches to assess specific needs (what types of tests—freestyle? dance? Moves in the Field?—and at what levels?) and the numbers of skaters who may want to test.
- Procure a block of ice time—ranging from several hours to several *days,* depending on the test session's likely size and needs.
- Determine the availability of judges and seal commitments from them for the duration of the session.
- Develop a test application with a fee schedule that will help offset the cost of hosting the session, and also distribute these test applications through skating coaches, bulletin boards, or direct mail.

- Arrange travel, food, and lodging for out-of-town judges.
- Collect test applications and fees and generate a test schedule that will include sufficient warm-up ice time for all skaters.
- Contact testing skaters and/or their pros to apprise them of the schedule well in advance of the actual testing date.
- Where possible, considering individual circumstances, accommodate skaters' requests for time and scheduling changes.
- Prepare necessary paperwork for judges to record scores and comments.
- Submit all needed paperwork to USFSA national headquarters.

The frequency with which any USFSA club holds test sessions varies greatly. Some clubs offer monthly test sessions, while others host only one or two per year. Still others may opt to hold none. If you'd like to test on a regular basis, you may have to travel to different clubs and rinks.

Skater Preparation for a USFSA Test Session

In order to be eligible for USFSA testing, you must be a member "in good standing" (meaning you have no outrageous outstanding debt) with your USFSA home club. If you wish to test at a rink other than your home club, be advised of the following:

- A host club determines whether it can or will accommodate testers from a different home club.
- Permission to test at a club other than your own must be granted by an officer from your home club.

Consult ahead of time with a skating professional regarding appropriate skating apparel. Different tests often require different looks. Polished skates, clean or new laces, and an overall well-groomed appearance are always suggested.

On the day of the test, arrive at the rink at least one hour before your scheduled test time. Due to scheduling glitches or scratches (a skater deciding not to test), the session may be running ahead or behind schedule.

You may warm up with other skaters in a small group on the ice, but when your turn comes to actually test, you'll have the rink all to yourself. In some situations—again depending on the type of test—you may have to share the ice with one other skater, who will usually be testing on the opposite side of the rink.

Most tests require the presence of three judges, although lower-level Moves in the Field, freestyle, and solo dance tests can be given with only one judge.

Judges may view your test while standing on the ice, sitting in the hockey box, or parked somewhere in the stands, depending on their own preferences. Each panel of judges will appoint a referee to communicate with you, the skater, on an as-needed basis. (For instance, at the conclusion of your test, the judges may want you to reskate an element—a spin or a jump or a section of footwork that they may have felt was weak during the test.) Each judge will have a clipboard and a test sheet to record marks and, sometimes, comments.

In all tests requiring three judges, only two of those three must give passing marks for you to succeed. The score sheets will read either "pass" or "retry." While you must wait 27 days before retrying, there are no limits on how many times you may attempt a particular test.

Upon the completion of the test, the club's test chairperson collects the judges' test sheets, tallies the scores, and (usually within 5 to 30 minutes) hands the sheets to the skaters and/or coaches.

This is the time when you're either apt to hear squeals of delight or see tears of disappointment, depending on the judges' decisions.

Although copies can be made (especially if it was a particularly well-skated test and you want a memento), the original sheets must be returned to the test chairperson for filing with the USFSA.

MENTAL PREPARATION FOR TESTING

Since it is a performance situation, testing can provoke the same nervousness and anxiety you might feel before a competition. To counteract the jitters, use the tools you learned in chapter 7:

- Visualize your test in your mind exactly the way you want it to be.

- Talk to yourself in a fashion that allows belief in success and positive outcome.
- Use relaxation exercises to settle your nerves.

Chapter 12 will deal specifically with mental tips for competition. Feel free to adapt them for a test situation. The Countdown to Competition sheet on page 149 may be especially helpful.

TO TEST OR NOT TO TEST

As with competition, the decision to test is ultimately your own. You can spend a lifetime on the ice and never have three individuals with clipboards critically evaluate your skating.

But if you're undecided, here are a few reasons you might want to consider test-taking:

- The ISI badge or USFSA certificate you can earn is a tangible touchstone, a record of accomplishment, and a potential motivator for future challenges to be faced in skating. For the young skater it is a welcome addition to his backpack or an open spot on his bedroom wall; something to show with pride to his friends and family members. For his parents, who are still learning the figure skating ropes, it is written proof that the child is progressing in the sport.
- Testing establishes credentials for a future employer should you decide at some point to pursue a skating or coaching career.
- Should you choose never to compete, testing is a way to push your own limits and compete solely with yourself.

CHAPTER 11

COMPETITION

I've been absolutely terrified every moment of my life—and I've never let it keep me from doing a single thing I wanted to do.

—Georgia O'Keefe

irst off, we want to be absolutely crystal clear about the notion of competitive skating. You can enjoy a lifetime of figure skating and never, ever enter a competition. Competition is not a given. Entering one or a thousand competitions should always be a well thought-out *choice*.

However, if you enjoy, or if you think you might enjoy, performing in front of an audience, consider competition. If you possess a competitive spirit, if you like to push your limits, go the distance, put yourself among many who are all going for the gold, figure skating in competition can add a thrilling dimension to your sport.

Competition is available for all ages and skill levels. You can participate in an ISI competition, a USFSA competition, or both. Although both offer a variety of options within the context of one organized competition, there are structural differences.

Let's explore what both organizations have to offer.

ISI COMPETITIONS

In order to participate in an ISI team competition you must:

- Be an individual member of ISI.
- Have your highest test registered with ISI headquarters.
- Represent an ISI member rink.

ISI competitions tend to offer more opportunities for recreational skaters to become involved in at least one of their scheduled events. (We'll define a *recreational skater* here as "one who, on the average, skates one to three times weekly.") Because skaters are awarded team points based on their placement in the various events, ISI competitions foster a sense of team spirit.

So as not to confuse you about the concept of an ISI team versus, say, a synchronized skating team, a bit more explanation is in order.

An ISI team is formed by a skating director who assembles interested skaters training in the same skating program or sharing ice time. The name of the team is determined by the rink manager or skating director, and is sometimes simply the name of the town where the team skates, or maybe something a little flashier like Blazing Blades or Podunk Poke-a-Longs.

Each team supplies a specific number of judges based on the number of skaters who participate at the competition. These judges must be current associate members of the ISI. They are almost always skating coaches, as opposed to the trained amateur judges used by the USFSA.

Although each skater is accumulating points for the team (which may result in the awarding of a first-place *team* trophy), most competitors would admit that their experience is one of vying for an *individual* medal.

Medals are usually awarded for first, second, and third place in each event. Although some competitions award medals for fourth place, usually ribbons are given to skaters who place fourth and fifth.

The number of competitors allowed in each group (also known as a flight) is limited to nine. This limited number increases the odds that more participants will be in medal and ribbon contention.

Each group is divided by age, ability level, and, in most cases, gender. Also, at an ISI competition the composition of your skating routine is restricted to the skating elements at or below your test level. In other words, if you're skating at an ISI Freestyle 1 level, don't even think about throwing in your triple lutz.

If you are the only entrant for a particular event, you can still compete. This is known as "competing against the book." In order to achieve a gold medal, you must score 80 percent out of 100 percent; 60 percent will get you a silver, 50 percent a bronze.

Events Offered at an ISI Competition

The variety of events offered at most ISI competitions supports the concept of "something for everybody" and the exploration of different avenues of skating. A *partial* listing of the different events, and a thumbnail sketch of what's involved in each, follows:

1. **Tots:** Designed for the preschooler who has limited on-ice experience. Some skills demonstrated in this event are: proper falling and getting up, marching in place, marching and moving, two-foot jump in place, beginning two-foot glide, standstill forward swizzle, backward wiggle, and lastly—skating with a dry diaper. (Just pulling your skating leg!)
2. **Beginning Skating:** Refer to the five different skills levels—Pre-Alpha, Alpha, Beta, Gamma, and Delta—as taught in chapter 6. All programs (the elements set to music) are one minute in duration, regardless of level, and must include one element from ISI Freestyle 1.
3. **Freestyle 1–10:** Again, refer to chapter 6 for the elements taught and required in Freestyle 1 through 3. All programs for Freestyle 1–3 are a minute and a half in length, plus or minus 10 seconds. See the ISI *Skaters and Coaches Handbook* for requirements for Freestyle 4–10.
4. **Creative Figures:** The running blade leaves a mark on the ice. In this event, then, skaters use their imaginations to create images on the ice—a flower, a letter of the alphabet, an animal.
5. **Pairs:** Requires a male and a female, both of whom have passed the ISI Delta test. Refer to the ISI *Skaters and Coaches Handbook* for details of the 10 levels.
6. **Couples:** A same-sex duo or a male-and-female couple (referred to as "couples mixed") who have passed the

Delta test. Refer to the ISI handbook for specifics for the 10 levels.

7. **Ice Dance—Solo and Partner:** A competitor must have passed the Delta test. Here again, there are 10 levels of Ice Dance. The first two levels demonstrate repetitions of basic dance steps performed to music (progressive sequences and swing rolls). The remaining levels consist of three or four of the compulsory dances as listed in the USFSA rulebook. In competition two or three of the sequences will be chosen at random by the competition director. Generally, the skaters are unaware of the choice until they actually arrive at the competition. You can compete with an opposite- or same-sex partner or dance solo. In shadow dance two skaters perform the same steps as close together as possible without actually touching.

8. **Special Skater:** This event is open to all skaters with physical and/or mental disabilities.

9. **Artistic Skating:** In this event you are afforded the opportunity to display strong edging, innovative moves and choreography, and unique musical interpretation. Artistic differs from Freestyle in that it emphasizes the command of the basic edges and originality. Jumps and spins are *not* the primary focus in this event but function more as a complement to the overall program. Competitions are usually limited to skaters who have attained Freestyle 3 or above. All programs are a minute and a half long.

10. **Comedy Team:** The number of skaters can range from 2 up to 14. Judges in the Comedy Team event look for humor, satire, and light or amusing characters and scenes. Costumes and props are essential. For all levels there is a two-minute time limit, plus or minus 10 seconds.

    Comedy Extravaganza (still under the auspices of this event) can host 15 or more skating in a group number to music. The time limit is three to four minutes.

11. **Interpretive:** The competition director chooses a piece of music, which remains a secret and unheard by the competitors up until the event. Skaters then listen to the music—three times—and must draw upon their creative powers to interpret it by constructing their own on-the-spot routines. Competitors are truly left to their own devices on this one, because coaches, friends, and family

members are prohibited from assisting them in any way in the invention of the skating program.

12. **Synchronized Skating Team:** A minimum of 8 and a maximum of 32 skaters perform in unison to music with a performance time limit of three to four and a half minutes. Refer to chapter 9 for details.

13. **Production Number:** This event involves an entire competitive team, with absolutely no limitations on the skating moves performed. A lavish, creative, artistic work marked by extreme freedom of style and structure using costumes and props. Production Numbers use 8 to 32 skaters and have a time limit of three to four and a half minutes. (Examples of productions we've seen: a send-up of *A Bug's Life,* a takeoff on the Wild West, and a three-ring circus.) Production Extravaganzas can have 33 or more skaters on the ice.

14. **Spotlight:** Skaters portray a character; we've seen famous athletes, toreadors, bumblebees, movie stars, celebrities, and cartoon characters. Spotlight can be performed solo or as a couple or family. Props are optional, but if used should help define the character. Spotlight levels correspond with ISI Freestyle levels. Pre-Alpha through Freestyle 3 skaters perform for one minute; Freestyle 4 through 10 skaters a minute and a half.

15. **Compulsories—Team and Solo:** Compulsories correspond to Freestyle levels 1 through 10. Before the competition, the competition director sends the skating directors of each team a list of three elements from each Freestyle level that must be combined into a short routine with minimal connecting moves. The routine is skated *without* music. Competitors are often limited to skating on only half the rink. They are judged on the technical quality of each element, including flow, posture, and correctness of execution.

16. **Footwork:** You must have passed the test for Freestyle 1 to be eligible to compete in a footwork event. Footwork entails a one-minute program comprised of an intricate step sequence set to music. Although the program may contain half-rotation jumps and spins of less than three rotations, the emphasis is on footwork itself—a variety of turns and controlled edges performed with quickness and speed. Levels correspond to Freestyle 1 through 10.

17. **Stroking:** Skaters perform a pattern of forward crossovers and basic forward stroking designed by the event referee. The music is selected by the competition director—usually a dance rhythm with an easily discernible beat.

USFSA COMPETITIONS

Within the USFSA there are two types of competitions—qualifying and invitational.

Qualifying competitions are generally for more accomplished skaters—serious competitors who are committed to training five or six days a week. Qualifiers are offered once yearly in the fall in nine different regions of the United States. (Here, in northeastern New York, skaters participate in the North Atlantics; California competitors are in either the Central Pacifics or the Southwest Pacifics.)

Those who place in the top three or four at the regional level qualify to progress to the sectional level of competition, of which there are three—Easterns, Midwesterns, and Pacific Coasts. Those skaters who finish at the top of their groups in sectionals then qualify to compete at the national level—called, aptly, the United States Nationals.

Skaters placing first, second, and third at the Senior level at U.S. Nationals may then represent the United States at the World Championships.

The locations of regional, sectional, and national competitions change from year to year, with USFSA clubs bidding to host the event. The site of the World Championship also varies from year to year.

Any USFSA club may host an *invitational* (also known as a non-qualifying) competition with a

BEGINNERS' COMPETITIONS

Even if you're still at the Basic Skills or beginning level, some clubs do offer low-key competitions for you. (The USFSA's name for this is Compete with U.S.) These events may be intraclub or invitational. Usually the competition involves you performing two or three maneuvers from your badge level, as determined by the competition director.

sanction from the national office. To participate, you must be a member in good standing with a USFSA club.

The competition director may place certain restrictions on skills allowed at the lower levels. For example, Preliminary skaters may be subdivided into two groups, with the competitors in one group allowed to perform axels and double jumps, while the other group is limited to single jumps only.

The Free Skate (Freestyle) levels usually offered at an invitational are:

1. No Test (the skater has passed no Freestyle tests beyond the Basic Skills program)
2. Pre-Preliminary
3. Preliminary
4. Pre-Juvenile
5. Juvenile
6. Intermediate
7. Novice
8. Junior
9. Senior

Events Offered at a USFSA Invitational Competition

Again, as with ISI competitions, the following is a *partial* listing of USFSA events, along with a short overview of each.

1. **Moves in the Field:** Skaters are divided by test level. The competition director will choose two or three specific patterns, which will be listed ahead of time on the competition application.
2. **Free skating or Freestyle:** Many different levels are offered, based on your test status. In USFSA free skating events, the content—the spins, jumps, and other "tricks"—of your program is unlimited. (Some skaters and coaches have been known to cram everything but the kitchen sink into a minute-and-a-half routine.) However, the competition director may limit multirevolution jumps (double axels, triple Salchows, and the like) at the lower levels if she so desires.
3. **Short Program:** Offered only at the Intermediate, Novice, Junior, and Senior levels, this event is often referred to as the technical program, because judges look for the techni-

cal quality you deliver when performing the designated elements. In this event you must perform six to eight required elements along with connecting steps to a passage of music. You are limited to *only* these elements, and each can be attempted only *once*. Technical programs are shorter in length than the free skating program, hence the term *short program*.

4. **Compulsory Program:** Usually offered at the lower levels—No test, Pre-Preliminary, Preliminary, Pre-Juvenile, and Juvenile. At the discretion of the competition director, five to seven skills may be listed on the competition application. These elements are not necessarily limited to jumps and spins; they may also include spirals, spread eagles, footwork sequences, or patterns from the Moves in the Field tests. These elements must be combined into a short routine with minimal connecting moves. (*Connecting moves* are arm movements and/or footwork used to enhance or interpret a certain phrase or passage of music. These moves can make a program more complex and interesting.) *No music is permitted,* and frequently the skater is asked to perform on only half the ice surface. The compulsory program can be viewed as a precursor to the short or technical program.

5. **Ice Dance:** In a nonqualifying competition there are usually a number of options for an ice dancer—partner dance, solo dance, and shadow dance. At all levels the specific compulsory dances that the skater must perform will be listed on the application form.

6. **Artistic Interpretive:** Here skaters listen to a piece of music chosen by the competition director and then spontaneously choreograph their own unique on-the-spot routine without assistance from coaches, family, or friends. This event is similar to the ISI's Interpretive.

7. **Showcase:** You perform a program that uses costume and choreography to depict the portrayal of a character. You may also use props to help identify and further define the character.

8. **Pair Skating:** Pairs competition is offered at the following levels: Preliminary, Juvenile, Intermediate, Novice, Junior, and Senior. Higher-level pairs may also skate a short program.

9. **Team Compulsories:** Skaters representing the same home club band together, and each skater performs one skill from a list chosen by the competition director.
10. **Spin Challenge:** The competition director chooses a specific spin; all competitors take to the ice simultaneously and, on cue, start spinning. The last competitor still spinning on a blade is the winner. (No points are given for the spinning in your head that you may feel for days afterward.)

ADULT COMPETITIONS

Many USFSA invitational competitions offer events *specifically* for adults. At ISI competitions, adults are simply integrated into the main body of the overall competition and placed within their own age groupings.

The age groupings for an adult specific USFSA competition are as follows:

Class 1: 25–35
Class 2: 36–45
Class 3: 46 and over

A NOTE FOR THE ADULT SKATER

In the last few years we've noticed a number of changes and additions to the skating world designed to serve the needs of the adult skater. Some rinks have adults-only public sessions. Some skating coaches now advertise that they work with adult students—exclusively or in addition to their younger figure skaters. Their teaching philosophies and techniques may be different for the grown-up who has decided to lace up a pair of skates and take to the ice. Lastly, a few summer programs are now offering adult weeks—training sessions specifically geared for those of us who pay taxes and worry about hair loss and middle-age spread.

Showing proof of age is required to compete, so this is not the place to claim that you are 39 for the fifth year in a row.

The adult skater wishing to qualify for national competition will have to follow an entirely separate series of qualifying competitions that ultimately lead to the U.S. *Adult* Nationals.

BUILDING A PROGRAM

Let's assume that after careful consideration you've decided to enter a competition. Time to lay that first cinder block.

We'll set this up as if you're going to skate an ISI Freestyle 1 program at a competition in the not-too-distant future. Besides simply reaching that level—and mastering the skating skills required in Freestyle 1—there are some other things you will need.

Program Music

If you're working with a coach, he may already have music cut on cassette tape, with just the right time requirements for Freestyle 1 and choreography to go with it. So just how did this wizard produce such a product with such astounding speed and accuracy?

It's recycled.

That's right, at some other time, before you, another one (or many!) of his students skated to that music. That student went on to higher Freestyle levels or dropped out of skating completely, so the program is open, ready to be used again. Your coach may suggest the type of skating outfit—the color and fabric—that goes well with the music, as he has probably seen both hits and misses in the past.

There is nothing wrong with this "program package"; it's convenient and takes some of the stress out of the whole affair. But if you decide that you want something that will be strictly your own, a program into which you can infuse your own unique personality, pick your own music. Or if you're working with a coach, negotiate a passage of music that is *you*—and that he'll be able to choreograph, too.

Your coach may have a warehouse full of tapes and CDs, so before you start running up your charge cards at the local music store, ask him if you can sort through his collection. Also solicit his opinion on what type of music would best suit your *style* of skating. (More on this matching process later.)

Your coach may have his own mixing board or computer software for cutting passages of music that will blend together into a nice little minute-and-a-half mix. If not, he'll send you, along with written suggestions or instructions, to a recording studio to have the music cut and mixed. Or he may go to the studio himself, alone, or perhaps accompany you to the session. If he comes with you, feel free to voice your thoughts and feelings as the tape is being cut and mixed. Again, this is a negotiation process. (In addition to recording studio time, your coach may charge you a fee for overseeing the operations.)

If you haven't hooked up with a pro for private lessons, you're in essence learning and progressing totally on your own. This affords you total freedom to choose your type of music and, later, the competition outfit you'll wear.

This final option has its advantages and disadvantages.

In USFSA freestyle skating you must avoid music with vocals. However, in the ISI Freestyle, Artistic, and Spotlight categories, vocals *may* be used—Bette Midler crooning "Wind Beneath My Wings" for Artistic, say, or John Travolta singing "Greased Lightning" from the musical *Grease* for a Spotlight number. To simplify things, here's an abbreviated list of the types of music from which you could select:

- Classical music—all varieties
- New Age music
- Traditional folk music
- Popular music from all eras (for instance, "Boogie Woogie Bugle Boy" from the 1940s, or a Beatles tune from the 1960s)
- World music
- Music from Broadway musicals, feature films, and TV shows

When searching for freestyle music, listen for selections with which you make an *emotional connection.* (After seeing the film *Schindler's List,* for example, Nikki felt compelled to work up a very moving program from her interpretation of certain passages of music from the movie.) In this way you're apt to come forth with a more meaningful, more expressive performance when the time comes.

Down through the years, the Schallehn sisters have skated freestyle to:

- The theme from the movie *Ice Castles* (*very* popular at one time)
- The theme from *Evita*—"Don't Cry for Me Argentina"
- Traditional South American music
- The theme from the TV program *The Addams Family*
- Music by Eric Tingstadt

. . . and this is just a partial list.

Many longer programs (over a minute-and-a-half) contain one or more changes of tempo. This can demonstrate to the judges your ability to interpret music and vary your skating style. Different pas-

MATCHING

Some skaters are diminutive little birds, their skates gently caressing the ice, arms moving like wings in flight. Other skaters are "power hitters"—well-muscled athletes who impress with strength, speed, the height of their huge jumps, and their speed-of-light spins. Each skater has a unique body type, style of skating, line, and presence on the ice. One of the worst things that sometimes occurs in competitive skating is a *mismatch* of music and skater.

Imagine this. A petite, lovely little lady takes to the ice. She's all frills, curls, and ruffles—her demeanor virtually screams, *"Perky!"* When her program music begins, though, out through the PA pours a bombastic classical score better suited for Conan the Barbarian. The poor kid looks petrified, scampering around the rink in a futile effort to keep up with the aural onslaught. In the end, a judge may be inclined to write: "Music too big."

When selecting program music, choose carefully. If your coach tries to thrust music on you that just doesn't feel right, go into your negotiation mode or request an alternative selection. You should always strive to *relate* to your music. A program at its worst is a bunch of required elements thrown against a background of mishmash music.

sages of music seem to suggest certain choreographed elements; for instance, a cymbal crash might be a great spot for a big jump, or a long elegant spiral corresponds beautifully to a slower regal piece of music. Judges love to see skaters dramatically change pace!

If working up a program is going to be a solo venture, the more traditional route would be to take your tapes and/or CDs into a recording studio and come up with a minute-and-a-half tape (ISI Freestyle 1) with the aid of an experienced sound engineer. Ask others in the skating community where they had their tapes cut—especially the ones that sound flawless over the PA. Make inquiry calls to local studios listed in the yellow pages. Be a good consumer, comparison shop, and—better yet—ask if the engineer has any experience cutting figure skating tapes.

Musicians on a budget never practice their songs in the studio. They have their tunes down cold before they ever set foot inside. They've learned that practicing in the studio can become very expensive, very quickly. Similarly, have a general idea of what you want before booking studio time. If you have a dual-dubbing cassette deck at home, make a rough cut and play it for the engineer so she has at least a notion of what you want as a finished product.

For our purposes, a *cut* is (hopefully) the seamless blending or merging of one passage of the music with another. Some cuts sound right; others are too abrupt, or the two pieces of music just don't mesh. The challenge is to get a near-seamless blend.

The *mix* is the final copy. Your engineer may boost the volume on some of the quieter, lower-range passages to equalize with the portions of your tape that naturally come through the speakers loud and brassy. Ask your engineer to mix the tape "hot"—with the overall volume boosted so you never need worry about hearing your tape through any PA system.

Ask for at least two master copies of your final mix. Make copies from the masters for practice and performance. Store your masters in a safe place. Label all your tapes with your name, your level, and any other information specified on your competition application.

Finally, on the top of your cassettes are two small tabs. With these tabs intact you can tape over the cassette with whatever music you desire.

Break the tabs! You don't ever want to risk someone recording *over* your program tape. (We've seen session supervisors accidentally hit the RECORD button on the tape deck rather than PLAY, only to erase the first 20 seconds and ruin the program tape.)

Competition Outfit

For females, you can find advertisements for competition dresses and dress makers in the pages of any of your skating magazines. However, some moms or local seamstresses can produce outfits that rival the larger companies. It's really a matter of choice and budget.

For you gentlemen out there, your competition garb choices are usually limited to pants and a shirt or a jumpsuit. A vest can be added, but jackets can be quite restrictive.

Types of materials can vary, and skating dresses go through certain fads and style changes. Some skaters are wearing crushed and flat velvet. Others prefer spandex, a material that moves with you. (Be careful when choosing sizes in spandex. A dress that is too large will sag and have flaps and folds; too small and it'll look like it was painted on.)

If a female is skating to "Rhapsody in Blue," most likely she's wearing a . . . ? Correct! A *blue* dress. This year Nikki's sister is skating to a medley of Spanish songs. Her dress is black and red, the top giving the appearance of a toreador's jacket.

If a male is skating to the music of *The Untouchables*, he might choose pin-striped pants, a white shirt, and suspenders—to visually add to the feel of the era and the music.

If you're working with a coach, she will usually have ideas and opinions regarding competition outfits. Some love dresses heavily beaded with rhinestones; others don't. Some have strong feelings about the neon colors that seem to fade in and out of popularity. And some coaches have an almost-phobic aversion to a particular color or fabric.

However, if you're putting a program together on your own, you can choose whatever cut, color, design, and material you desire. Soliciting a friend or family member's opinion might be helpful before making your final choice.

Competition Application

The next two questions you'll have to answer are *where* and *when* to compete. Both the ISI and USFSA magazines list the dates and locations of endorsed events, as well as a contact person's phone number. Skating club and rink bulletin boards often offer flyers and brochures advertising upcoming competitions. If you're taking private lessons, ask your coach if he knows of any soon-to-be-held competitions either in or out of the area.

Once you locate an application form for a competition that fits with your time frame and skating budget, enter all necessary biographical info, get the required signatures (coach, club official), check off what event(s) you wish to enter, scribble out a check, throw it all in an envelope (sometimes a self-addressed, stamped envelope is required), affix postage, and mail.

COMPETITION CHECKLIST

Preparedness can help combat some of the chaos that may come with competition. Feeling confident that are you ready in terms of equipment and accessories will help you focus solely on your skating. (Mental preparations will be covered in the next chapter.)

Clothing

Before leaving for the competition, check your outfit for any rips, tears, or holes—and make sure it fits properly (the thong look created by a too-small dress is not a popular choice with judges). Tights are notorious for taking on runs or rips. As such, it's wise to own a backup outfit and extra pairs of tights. If you choose to wear undergarments, make sure they don't peek out from underneath or show through your dress. Most female skaters wear a warm-up sweater, so pull that from your closet as well.

For competition, male skaters often wear pants (sometimes elasticized) with a subdued or showy shirt (depending on personality and the program to be skated), or a jumpsuit constructed from one of many material choices. Again, the same suggestions apply—check for flaws in the material and choose backups.

Skate Boots

Dirty boots are a pet peeve of many coaches and judges. To avoid matching a gorgeous new skating outfit with filthy skates, here's the drill:

1. Use a soft cloth or cotton balls soaked in rubbing alcohol or nail polish remover to erase any marks or stains on your boots.
2. Next, apply a quality skate polish to really make those puppies shine! (Your best bets are the brands marketed by the various boot manufacturers—Harlick, SP-Teri, and so on. In a pinch you can use the polish sold in supermarkets for baby shoes or nurses' footwear.)
3. Finally, if your once-white skate laces now range anywhere from a dingy gray to a midnight black, replace them!

Skate Bag

Okay, so you've determined that you have an outfit that fits and is devoid of any stray moth holes or rips the size of Montana. Your skates have been restored to a nicer shade of white (black for you guys). Now you're ready to pack your skate bag.

- **Skates:** Truly! We can name more than a few skaters who have forgotten their most important possessions, arriving at a competition only to be seized with absolute panic. Bottom line—no skates, no competition.
- **Skate guards.**
- **Towel and soakers:** Soakers are terry cloth coverings for your blades. They're primarily for moisture control, not to be walked in.
- **Polish:** For any last-minute touch-ups. Wrap this in a plastic bag to prevent polishing everything in your skate bag.
- **Extra pairs of laces:** You never know when your laces might quit on you. Make sure the ones you pack are the right length. They won't do you any good if they lace only halfway up your boots.
- **Two copies of your program tape:** One to hand in at the registration desk, and a backup to keep in your bag or to have your coach hold just in case the cassette player at the competition decides to eat your first copy, or it inadvertently gets lost. Before packing make sure that the playing time (one minute, two minutes, or whatever) is in compliance with event guidelines and that the tapes are labeled according to competition rules. Transport the

tapes in their clear plastic cases and/or place them in a separate storage box within your skate bag to ensure that they're protected. If you've entered more than one event, each event has different program music. The same rule applies: Have a backup for each copy you hand in at the registration desk.

- **Two pairs of gloves.**

Garment Bag

You paid hard-earned cash for your skating outfit; you don't want it to arrive at a competition looking wrinkled. The solution is simple—purchase a garment bag or two.

Here's what to (carefully) place inside:

- **One or more competition outfits:** In addition to having a backup, some skaters wear different dresses (or shirts and pants for the guys) for each separate event (Freestyle, Artistic, Interpretive) they've entered. This is optional, but not mandatory, especially if you're on a budget.
- **Practice dress for females, practice shirt for males:** Again, this isn't mandatory, but if you've purchased a practice session before your event, you may want to wear something other than your most dazzling ensemble to sweat in. For females, a leotard paired with a chiffon dancer's wraparound skirt will work just fine.
- **Warm-up sweater.**
- **Extra street clothes:** No matter how ravishing you look in that sequined garb, eventually you may want to change out of your competition clothes and into something fresh (other than what you wore for the trip), especially if you go out somewhere to celebrate your medal win.
- **Makeup and hair accessories:** Place these in the bottom of your garment bag, or pack them in a separate bag. Competing with bed-head is not recommended. Be advised that in competition an overall well-groomed look can only add to your on-ice presence.

Lastly, somewhere deep inside *you*, pack your sense of enthusiasm for the new adventure you're about to experience.

CHAPTER 12

MENTAL TIPS FOR COMPETITION

All of the significant battles are waged within the self.

—Sheldon Kopp

Arriving at your first competition, you can expect to feel a wealth of emotions, some pleasant, some not so pleasant. Along with your excitement, you'll probably feel some anxiety about actually getting out there and strutting your stuff. A little voice inside you might ask, "Why did we ever sign up for this?" This is normal.

The way to lessen your anxiety and maximize your competition enjoyment is to learn to recognize and control the stress—both external and internal.

Let's start by learning to either roll with or control the external stressors.

If your competition is out of town, an hour or two away, allow yourself plenty of time for travel. Arriving with only minutes to spare before your scheduled event will result in a huge spike in your anxiety level. If you arrive late, you will miss your event and the opportunity to compete entirely. Unless you're a millionaire skating superstar, the organizers of the competition will *not* wait for you. Most event organizers (and coaches) advise that you arrive at the rink at least *one hour* before your scheduled event. This should give you enough time to check in, change, warm up (off the ice), and do some last-minute mental tuning.

Once you're at the rink or arena, the first place you want to locate (after the rest rooms) is the registration desk. The volunteers at this desk will be friendly and helpful, or grumpy, or anywhere in between.

If you encounter the crabby type(s), roll with it, and don't let it diminish your enthusiasm for your upcoming event. At most competitions, this desk is where you turn in your program cassette. (Make sure it is rewound all the way back onto the clear leader.) In return, the registration people will hand you a packet that *may* include a program of scheduled events (a thrill to see your name in print!), a keychain, pen, pencil, or terry cloth skating towel (the absolute best freebie), some discount coupons for fast food or skating apparel, and other such goodies.

Then ask the location of your locker room.

If it's time to change into your competition outfit and pull on your skates, do so. Otherwise, depending on your comfort level, you can leave your gear in the locker room or shoulder your skate and garment bags and check out the happenings in other parts of the rink.

Sometimes events are running ahead of schedule; sometimes they're running behind. (One year at a Regional competition, Nikki was in a "flight" with 15 other girls and didn't step onto the ice until close to 11 o'clock at night!)

Other annoyances may occur. For example, some competitions run the Zamboni religiously after several events with large flights of skaters. However, we were once at a competition where an entire afternoon passed, scores of skaters had chipped and shredded the ice, and the Zamboni never came out of the garage. Nikki ended up skating on a surface that held deep gouges, holes, and ruts.

Again, this is an external stressor—something that, if it occurs at your competition, you'll have to accept and do the very best with the ice surface you're given.

If a competition is out of town, some skaters prefer to arrive the day before and spend the night in a motel. Their scheduled event may be at 8 o'clock the next morning; an overnight makes more sense than driving on unknown roads in the wee hours of the morning.

Other skaters arrive the day before to get the feel of the area and acclimate themselves to the rink or arena. If you have the funds for a room and meals, treat yourself. Go shopping, buy some trinkets, and visit the rink to learn the layout. Sit in the stands and visualize yourself skating your event, performing well in all your elements.

The major downside to having too much time before your event is the possibility that large blocks of unstructured time may be fertile ground for the emergence of the "what ifs." *What if* I forget the elements in my program? *What if* the other skaters are better than me? *What if* I fall?

For your use, we've included two Countdown to Competition sheets to structure your time before your event. We've filled out the first with sample activities. The second is blank.

COUNTDOWN TO COMPETITION

Event time: 3:00 p.m.

3 Hours Before . . .
Have a nice lunch with Mom. Drink water—no cola or beverages with caffeine.

2 Hours Before . . .
Listen to Goo Goo Dolls, Matchbox 20, and Brandy on my Walkman.

1 Hour Before . . .
Arrive at rink, check in, locate locker room, find my coach. Jump rope for 10 minutes. Listen to program tape on my Walkman. Visualize doing my best.

Half an Hour Before . . .
Do light stretching. Short relaxation exercise. Repeat positive affirmations to myself.

A Few Minutes Before Warm-Up . . .
Recite cue phrase—"I love to skate"—to myself.
Recite cue word—*"Yes!"*
Shoulders back, head up—*"Win/win at warm-up!"*

COUNTDOWN TO COMPETITION

Event time: _____

_____

3 Hours Before . . .

_____

2 Hours Before . . .

_____

1 Hour Before . . .

_____

Half an Hour Before . . .

_____

A Few Minutes Before Warm-Up . . .

WIN/WIN AT WARM-UP

When your event finally nears, you should be close to the edge of the ice. An ice captain, a volunteer with a clipboard and perhaps a walkie-talkie, will call out your name to make sure you are present and accounted for to skate. ("Here!" is your desired response. "Yo" sounds a bit cocky.) Soon the announcer, over the PA, will call your name, as well as those of the others in your flight, to "take the ice for warm-up."

Here's where things can get a little dicey.

First and foremost, when you're called—*remember to remove your skate guards.* If you step onto the ice with those guards on, you'll go down, fast, lickety-split. Falling flat on your butt right out of the gate does not make for an auspicious beginning.

If you're able *without being a hazard,* try to get out fast and lead the pack for the first pass at forward stroking.

You and your coach will probably have a set pattern of elements to practice during warm-up. Your coach may be watching from the side, calling out instructions to you. Keep in mind that you are on the ice with some very high-spirited skaters, all of them itching to do well in warm-up and performance. Although your peripheral vision keeps track of when skaters may be drawing near, on competition day, exercise a bit more caution. It's the skater's equivalent of driving defensively.

The mental tip we'd now like to pass on to you is called Win/Win at Warm-Up. It goes like this: If you have a fantastic warm-up, land all your jumps (if your program has jumps), execute fast and centered spins, and complete all required elements for your routine, tell yourself—"As I did it in warm-up, so too I'll do it in performance."

If, perchance, the fates are against you in warm-up and you manage to blow all your jumps; you spin lopsided, twirling like a broken top; and in general your required elements are sloppy, without presence, or just downright tragic—tell yourself, "Okay, I've got all the bugs and mistakes worked out of my system. *Now* I'm ready for truly great performance."

With this *positive* interpretation of either situation, no matter what happens at warm-up it's a "win-win" situation.

After the allotted time for warm-up ends, you'll be asked to clear the ice. You'll stand near the other competitors waiting for your turn. The order of skating is determined randomly; you might be first, last, or somewhere in the middle. If you have to wait, please avoid any skaters who are making a meal out of their fingernails or curled into a fetal position on one of the benches.

You can listen to music on your headphones, do deep knee bends, talk, make jokes with your coach, stare at the wall, or do some last-minute mental fine-tuning. Some coaches advise their skaters not to watch the performer on the ice. Other coaches don't perceive this as a problem. Check with your coach, experiment, and see what works best for you. The point here is to avoid any *external* stressor that could potentially distract you or push your level of stimulation into the red zone.

Now let's tackle the *internal* stressors that could take away from your enjoyment of a competition.

CONTROLLING INTERNAL STRESS

As you walk into the rink on competition day, take a deep breath, hold it, exhale, and think, "Relax and enjoy." Adopt an attitude of gratitude. Be thankful that you've got the health, the strength, the finances to pursue such an activity.

Once you're in the rink, it'll be important to pay attention to, and monitor where, you fall within your "performance zone."

Think of a gauge, a meter, in the shape of a horizontal half circle. Within this gauge is an indicator needle. In terms of activation, arousal, or stimulation on your nervous system, when you're asleep, the needle is lying flat on the left-hand side. You get up, have a cup of coffee, pour yourself a bowl of flakes. The needle starts to come up a bit; your nervous system is awakening.

Think of dead center, when the needle is straight up and down, as your peak performance zone. When you're in your zone, your body is relaxed but ready, your mind is alert and clear. If the needle starts to creep over toward the right, you're now entering the red zone. Muscles may start to clench or quiver; your mind may race or swirl like a possessed merry-go-round. You feel nervous and scared.

If at any point while you're awaiting your time on the ice you begin to enter the red zone, there are several strategies you can use to bring yourself back to the peak performance zone.

Active Strategies

- Any form of physical exercise can rid your body of unwanted stress or tension. Keep a jump rope in your skate bag and haul it out if you're starting to feel too tense. Stretching, calisthenics, and running in place can all bring you back down to your desired state of arousal.
- Play air guitar or sing along to the music coming from your Walkman.
- Chew gum vigorously. Various studies support many sport psychologists' claims that facial muscles control the degree of tension in the entire body. After chewing gum the facial muscles are a bit exhausted, and the jaw slackens. (Remember to dispose of it before you skate.)
- Belly-breathe. Take oxygen deep into your lungs so your belly rises before your chest. (This is not the time to be

vain. So it looks a little weird.) When you take shallow breaths, carbon dioxide builds up in your brain and may impair concentration and coordination.

- If you notice that your hands are clenched into fists, uncurl them and literally shake them loose.
- Talk, laugh, and gossip with family, friends, or coach.

Passive Strategies

- Perform relaxation exercises, like the procedures described in chapter 5 or recorded on tape. There are dozens of types of relaxation techniques on tape. Pay a visit to your tape or CD store or place an order from a self-help catalog.
- With your eyes closed, visualize a tranquil scene—floating on a raft in a pool, basking on the beach, watching a sunrise or a sunset. It's a moment of "remembered peacefulness," as Norman Vincent Peale termed it.
- Listen to soft, soothing classical or New Age music. A wide selection is available from your tape and CD retailer.

It may be necessary to move away from the chaos in the halls and locker rooms to perform passive or active relaxation techniques, because these external stressors contribute to or cause internal stress. Sequester yourself high in the stands or bleachers or take a walk outside and find a quiet place near the building.

Your efforts will be rewarded with a more enjoyable and controlled skating experience.

Lastly

If you're up there in the stands, pop a spare copy of your program tape into your Walkman and visualize yourself performing in an associated fashion. (Remember, associated is when you imagine yourself *actually there*—you feel your edges gripping into the ice; feel the movement of your arms, legs, and torso; hear the sound of your blades on the ice and the claps, whistles, and shouts of encouragement from your family, friends, and coach.)

Have several 3- by 5-inch index cards on which you've written some positive affirmations. ("I can feel calm, confident, and assured"; "I want to show the audience my passion for skating"; "Soon the ice will be all mine!") Study them. Take them into your mind and your heart.

RECOVERING FROM FALLS IN COMPETITION

You've practiced your program dozens of times. You feel physically and mentally ready. You've had your warm-up, an eternity of time seems to pass, and then finally it's your turn to skate. You take to the ice, spurred on by the cheers and applause of your family and friends. Confidently, you glide out to your designated spot in the rink and strike your beginning pose, your music begins, and you're skating. . . .

And then the unexpected occurs. You set up for a jump, perhaps one of your easiest, execute your takeoff, and become airborne—only to miss your landing and crumple to a heap on the ice. How you handle this unplanned event may have a dramatic impact on the rest of your performance and even your placement in the scoring.

You first need to be aware of the concept of recovery. For our purposes here, we'll define *recovery* as "an act or gesture of refocusing that results in completion of the skating program, often with renewed vigor, energy, and vitality." After a fall, you'll need to concern yourself with two types of recovery—physical and mental. The two are interwoven.

Physical Recovery

No one likes to see a fallen skater linger on the ice. We've sat through competitions and shows in which an audience practically pleaded with a downed skater to get back on his or her feet. The collective groan you hear emitted from the crowd is evidence that, they too, are saddened by your mishap. *But now they want to see redemption!* It is critical that you rebound from the ice as quickly as you can. Scramble to your feet, put a smile on your face, and exude confidence, competence, and control. Lead the crowd, the judges, your friends, your family to believe that, literally, *you've put that fall behind you* and you're moving on to the rest of your program.

Mental Recovery: The Inner Dialogue

So just how *do* you shake off the rattle and disappointment and go on to skate a superlative performance? The answer lies within what you say to yourself as soon as it registers that you've fallen. How you talk to yourself, the tone and timbre of your inner voice, is also a critical component in mental recovery. Here are some examples of inner dialogues culled from our work with successful recoverers:

- "Ouch! That certainly woke me up! My focus will be sharper now." (Spoken in a humorous tone.)
- "Oops—better land the next one!" (Again, the inner voice is light, buoyant, and with a tinge of humor.)
- "Calm—it's okay—keep moving." (Perhaps hearing your coach's voice in your head or your own voice, soothing but strong.)
- "It's behind me—it's gone!" (Spoken to yourself as you regain your footing in a modulated, confident, even tone of voice.)

Your inner dialogue should always avoid *catastrophizing* and *analyzing*. An example of catastrophizing a fall would be: "Oh my God, this is the *worst* thing that could ever happen. Now my *entire* program is blown. I *know* the judges will put me in last place. I'll *never* be able to get over this. All this hard work down the drain . . . my coach will drop me, my parents disown me. . . ."

Notice that a catastrophizing statement tends to have a certain runaway quality to it. The generalizations, the use of irrational absolutes (*entire, know, never*) only adds fuel to the anxiety fire. You're still lamenting the fall well into your next element. A frightened, haunted look often seizes your face. You begin "skating scared," with muscles stiffened in fear.

An example of analyzing a fall in freestyle would be: "I've landed that jump hundreds of times in practice. What went wrong? Maybe it was the way I set it up. Did I overrotate? Was I too tilted in the air? Did I . . . ?"

If you analyze a missed jump, we in the stands see you wearing a quizzical, sometimes spacey look on your face. In this situation the attempt to "figure out the fall" rather than move on to the rest of the performance often results in a loss of focus and concentration. Save analysis for after the event with your coach and/or video playback.

During your next practice session, tune in to what you say to yourself should you fall on a jump during a run-through of your program. If you're catastrophizing or analyzing, *stop*. Instead, begin installing new self-statements about the mishap of falling. Experiment until you get the most effective wording and language that will:

- Compartmentalize the error. Remember, the mistake is only one speck, one slight snag in the overall breadth of your entire performance.
- Seed feelings of humor, hope, and optimism.

Finally, realize that all skaters, at one time or another, fall on jumps during a performance situation. *The difference that will make the difference is how you respond.*

We'll end where we began—with the sense of ambivalence you might feel in regard to entering a competition. Some psychologists refer to it as the "approach-avoid syndrome."

In Tibet, Buddhist monk novitiates must pass through the Hall of a Thousand Terrors before they can enter into the Room of Enlightenment. The terrors are always the novitiates' own worst *personal* fears and anxieties. And although the terrors aren't really real, they *feel* and *appear* real to the young novitiates.

Once the novitiate enters the Hall of a Thousand Terrors there is no turning back, as the door is locked behind them and the only way out is straight ahead and into the wondrous Room of Enlightenment.

For centuries now, as nervous novitiates await their turn to enter into the Hall, eventually to make their way to Enlightenment, they turn and ask advice of the sage old monks who stand there watching.

For centuries the advice has always been the same.

"Just keep your feet moving . . ."

CHAPTER 13

OFF-ICE TRAINING

We must never escape the obligation of living at our best.

—Janet Erskine Stuart

Many skaters have asked us if there are other activities that would supplement and/or accelerate the acquisition and maintenance of skating skills. The answer is yes. But always keep in mind that the best way to be a better skater is simply to skate, putting in productive time at the rink. Writers write, drummers drum, plumbers plumb, skaters skate.

Your general level of fitness will be the greatest attribute (along with your self-confidence and enthusiasm) that you can bring to the rink. Good cardiovascular health and upper- and lower-body strength will all contribute to building a smoother, stronger skater.

As such, there are a number of other sports, physical exercises, and cross-training activities that will improve cardiovascular functioning and general body toning.

Some simulate, or come close to simulating, the muscle movements needed for stroking, jumping, and spinning, while others don't.

We've compiled a list.

In-Line Skating

Skating on Rollerblades not only builds your cardiovascular system but also simulates the stroking action and movement of ice skating. On in-line skates you can perform forward and backward stroking as well as forward and backward crossovers. You'll also build leg and lower-body strength and fine-tune your sense of balance.

As always, safety first. Asphalt is unforgiving. Wear a helmet, and wear knee, wrist, and elbow pads. School parking lots (in the off hours), state parks, bike paths, and indoor roller-skating rinks are often good places to in-line skate—but check first to make sure it's allowed. Skating in the street presents many hazards, including traffic and gutters that are often littered with stones and broken glass. Such debris can catch in a wheel and quickly throw you.

Slideboards

A *slideboard* is a 6- or 8-foot strip of thin, slippery plastic with wooden or plastic stops on the ends. To use one, you slip on a pair of cloth booties and push back and forth along the strip, alternating your pushing foot and gliding foot. This training device was first used by speed skaters, but it's perfectly acceptable for the figure skater to build foot and leg strength and as a cardiovascular exercise.

Slideboards were faddish within the aerobics community for a while and could be purchased in sporting goods and large department stores. Their popularity, however, seems to have waned, and slideboards can be difficult, but not impossible, to locate.

Trampolines and Jump Ropes

Trampolines for home use come in two varieties—mini tramps that run about 28 inches in diameter, and larger models, which can run 12 to 14 feet in diameter. Some rinks and summer programs use the industrial model—the heavy-duty type used by amateur and professional gymnasts.

The cross-training benefits of using a trampoline to improve your figure skating skills appear to be threefold. First, the trampoline acclimates you to being airborne, executing revolutions, and breaking the bonds of gravity for a few seconds. Second, it strengthens the muscles used in figure skating jumps; some skating programs are now boasting an increase in the percentage of "vertical lift" of the on-ice jumps of skaters who incorporate trampoline bouncing into their overall training. Third, extended periods of time spent jumping may increase your cardiovascular capacity.

Trampolines are not toys. Should you purchase one for cross training at home, heed the manufacturer's instructions and warnings for its use.

Before a session, a test, or a competition, you're sure to see some skaters jumping rope in lobbies and locker rooms. In addition to warming up the muscles used for jumping, it helps you focus on the spring you need to lift up into the air. For test and competition situations, it's also an easy and convenient way to jump away any jitters or nervousness.

Plyometrics

Originating in Europe, plyometrics or "jump training" first caught the attention of American coaches and athletes when early-1970s Eastern European athletes were turning into the powerhouses of international sports. Plyometrics have been used to improve performance in figure skating, weight lifting, track and field, gymnastics, baseball, softball, basketball, cycling, diving, skiing, football, and rowing.

Specific plyometric exercises for figure skating may include repetitions of jumps up onto wooden plyometric boxes of varying sizes, jumping onto padded mats, or repeated side-to-side jumps between small plastic cones that serve as borders.

Plyometrics purportedly works by attempting to allow a muscle to obtain optimal strength in as little time as possible. For figure skating, the desired outcome is *explosive* jumping power.

Check your rink bulletin boards for flyers advertising plyometric classes, or contact local gyms or personal trainers to inquire whether they offer the exercises in group or individual sessions. Lastly, there are several instructional books on the market if you want to read more about plyometrics or attempt training on a solo basis.

Weight Training and Working Out at a Gym

We're not proposing that you bulk up to the size of a Schwarzenegger. Many beginners truly do fear that working out with weight and gym equipment will result in packing on incredible amounts of muscle.

Not true. Not all muscle is bulky. Your body is equipped with a diverse range of muscle fibers. While bodybuilders and powerlifters do have muscles grown thick with exercise, some muscles (called slow-twitch) do not respond to exercise with growth. Work with a trainer who can devise sport-specific exercises. A proper weight-training routine can help you reduce fat and tone muscles without adding dense muscle mass.

We consulted with Michael Braet, the trainer at the gym where Nikki and her sister work out. For their sport-specific training, Mike devised a number of exercises to assist in maintaining and building their on-ice skills.

We'd like to share with you the core exercises of this workout:

- Leg presses
- Leg extensions
- Leg curls
- Calf presses
- Chest presses
- Flyes
- Shoulder presses
- Lateral raises
- Triceps push-downs
- Lat pull-downs
- Rowing
- Shrugs
- Bicep curls
- Abdominal crunches

For your cardio training, consider low-impact aerobics classes (if held at the gym), stationary bike riding, Stairmasters, elliptical trainers (you'll feel like you're snowshoeing or cross-country skiing), or fast walking on a treadmill. Realize that all these recommended exercises are considered low impact for your knees. In our opinion, the constant pounding your knees receive when jogging or

CHOOSING A GYM OR HEALTH CLUB

Most reputable gyms and health clubs will offer you a free trial membership. In this way you can ascertain the feel and personality of the facility. Here are some things to look for in any gym or health club:

- Machines that work and are well serviced.
- Staff members who are credentialed and well versed in sport-specific training. Minimally, trainers should be CPR and first-aid certified. Inquire as to whether they have degrees in the fitness field and/or national personal training certification. Look for credentials or certification from the National Strength and Conditioning Association, the American College of Sports Medicine, the American Council on Exercise, and the National Academy of Sports Medicine. (In Mike Braet's opinion, the National Strength and Conditioning Association certification should be your credential of choice when choosing a trainer.)
- Relatively short waiting times for machines and free weights.
- An upbeat and friendly atmosphere—staff and members alike.
- Sanitary bathroom and shower facilities.

If you would rather set up a home gym in your basement or spare room, Mike recommends that you minimally equip it with:

- A fully adjustable weight bench (flat up to 90 degrees)
- Adjustable dumbbells with spin collars
- A weighted pulley unit with leg attachments

After purchasing and setting up your equipment, hire a personal trainer to *at least* establish your initial routine and teach you proper exercise technique.

running could ultimately be injurious to them. Remember, in figure skating your knees are priceless. We thus advise you to avoid running as an exercise, especially the long-distance variety.

Dance

Ballet can help to improve your posture, carriage, and presentation, along with increasing strength and flexibility. As a spectator, you can in some cases tell that a skater has had prior (or supplemental) ballet training: His or her "touch" and execution of elements will seem softer, more graceful and fluid.

Jazz, tap, modern, and hip-hop are the types of dancing you see most often in current music videos. Swing has recently become popular as well; ice interpretations of this form of dance have already made their way into amateur and professional skating routines. All can be lively, quick, sassy, and seductive. As with other types of dance, they can increase your strength and flexibility if you commit to practicing on a regular basis. If you tend to be somewhat inhibited on the ice, many of these dance disciplines can help bring you out of your shell. If you are competing and your program music has a contemporary feel to it, training in jazz and hip-hop may give you a distinct advantage in presentation.

Still, *any* kind of dance (even just moving to music from your CD player in the living room) can help you feel the beats and relate to the music. Too many skaters simply reel off their required elements while their music plays in the background. The performance comes across as flat, cold, and sterile. In *your* actual ice performances, on the other hand, we want you to be in sync with the music, letting it flow through you, interpreting the drama, passion, and changes in tempo with your entire body.

So in the words of Zorba the Greek—*"Dance!"*

Skate Spinners

In the pages of your skating magazines you may find advertisements for two types of *skate spinners*—off-ice training devices intended to perfect the quality and speed of your spins.

Type 1 is a piece of hard rectangular plastic approximately 9 by 3 inches with a slightly curved bottom. Find a bare square of linoleum or a polished wood floor, put one foot on the spinner, and execute a spin. The manufacturer claims that this device simulates the feel of an on-ice spin. It's endorsed by some skating professionals, though other coaches with whom we've spoken aren't that impressed. The device retails for about $30 to $35.

Type 2 consists of two square pieces of metal, covered with a rubberized material, with ball bearings sandwiched between. This spinner can be used on linoleum, wood, or carpet. As with any product, it has both supporters and detractors. It retails for approximately $35 to $40.

NUTRITION AND GENERAL HEALTH CONSIDERATIONS

We don't claim to be nutritionists or health educators, but consider the following scenario.

Imagine that you invest your life savings in a thoroughbred racehorse. After taking the animal home, you proceed to feed him a steady diet of junk food and keep him up late at night smoking, drinking hard liquor, and playing poker.

Where do you think your horse will place in his first race?

Right: dead last.

What you eat and your off-ice activities will influence your on-ice performance. Indulge in an unbalanced diet, put yourself into sleep deficit, and watch how you will have to literally drag yourself across the ice. If skating is important to you and you've set specific training and performance goals for yourself, remaining mindful of nutrition, weight, and sleep requirements is essential.

If you need assistance with your diet, consult with your personal physician, a nutritionist, or a registered dietitian.

CHAPTER 14

AS A SPECTATOR

Joy is but the sign that creative emotion is fulfilling its purpose.

—Charles DuBois

If you're an avid figure skating fan, you'll probably be spending your downtime—when you're not actively practicing your individual elements or entire program—channel-surfing in search of TV coverage of a skating event or scrounging up a few bucks for a ticket to a live show or competition that will soon be rolling into your town.

In this chapter we'll help you become a gold-medal spectator.

Here's what you'll be looking for in amateur competition at the National, World, and Olympic level.

THE SHORT

In both men's and ladies' singles (freestyle) skating, competitors begin by performing the technical or "short" program. The short program runs 2 minutes and 40 seconds and contains eight different required elements with connecting steps. These required elements are the *only* ones that can be in the program, and each element can be attempted only *once*.

Required Elements—Men's Short

- A double or triple axel
- Footwork or step sequence leading into a triple or quadruple jump
- A jump combination consisting of two triple jumps or a double and a triple jump
- A flying spin with at least eight revolutions
- A camel spin or sit spin with only one change of foot; at least six revolutions
- A spin combination with at least two changes of position but only one change of foot, and six revolutions on each foot (for example, a camel spin to a back camel to a back sit spin)
- Two different footwork sequences forming a straight line, circle, or serpentine pattern

Required elements—Ladies' Short

- A double axel
- Footwork or step sequence leading into a double or triple jump
- A jump combination consisting of two triple jumps or a double and a triple jump
- A flying spin with a minimum of eight revolutions
- A layback or "sideways-leaning" spin with a minimum of eight revolutions
- Spin combinations with only one change of foot but at least two changes of position, and a minimum of six revolutions on each foot
- A spiral step sequence that covers the ice in a circular, oval, or serpentine pattern
- A straight line, circular, or serpentine step sequence

For both men and women, the elements can be performed in any order desired. Some competitors choose to perform their most difficult elements toward the beginning. This strategy serves to get the tough stuff out of the way so they can relax (sort of) and attack the rest of the program—featuring their favorite tricks—with the confidence of knowing that their most challenging maneuvers are completed.

Other skaters prefer to let their nerves settle in and their focus take hold before attempting the elements they find most formidable. The downside of this waiting strategy, however, is that the more time elapses, the more the skater risks running out of energy—the very energy required to lift off into a required double or triple, or snap into a nice tight spin.

JUDGING THE SHORT

Judges mark skaters on a six-point scale, with 6.0 being the best possible score. Two separate marks are given to each skater, the first being for *required elements,* and the second for *presentation.*

The technical marks (for required elements) awarded by the judges are based on the following aspects of the skater's performance:

- The technical correctness of the jumps, including height, air position, completed rotation, and proper takeoff and landing edge—plus the difficulty of the jumps in comparison with those performed by other competitors.
- The quality of the spinning positions—including arched back, pointed toes, and raised head—speed of the spins, number of revolutions, and accurateness and degree of center on the spin versus one that travels across the ice.
- The intricacy, difficulty, and edge quality of the footwork sequences. Also, the speed and posture with which sequences are performed, and whether they match with and reflect the cadence of the program music.
- The overall speed and difficulty of the skating routine.

The judge's mark for presentation considers the following aspect of the routine:

- Choreography
- Posture and carriage
- Speed and flow
- Creativity

continued

- Interpretation of the music
- Ability to cover the entire ice surface
- Level of confidence exuded by the skater

Specific deductions are made for mistakes in jumps, spins, and footwork. The magnitude of the deduction is based on the severity of the error and will range from 0.1 up to 0.5 point, with the greatest deduction being for the complete omission of an element.

Marks given for presentation tend to be more subjective, based on individual judges' connection with the program and how appealing, or unappealing, they find the overall routine.

A skater's placement in the short program counts for one third of his final standing. On network TV you might only see the top six or seven skaters in the event, whereas cable may show more of the flight (the field of skaters).

THE LONG

The Free skate or long program is the final phase of both male and female singles competition. The ladies skate a four-minute routine, and the men a four-and-a-half-minute. In the long program, anything goes! Skaters tend to load their long programs with as many triple and (perhaps) quadruple jumps as they believe they can execute.

There are recommendations as to what elements should be included in the long:

- At least one but not more than three jump combinations
- At least four different spins
- A limited number of performances of the *same* jump
- Suggested footwork sequences

But there are no specific deductions for program content.

There is a freedom in the long not seen in the short. Elements *can* be retried if the first attempt resulted in a poor or unsuccessful completion.

Skaters will sometimes adjust their programs as they perform to match or outdo a competitor who has skated before them. In an attempt to skate cleanly, competitors might deliberately omit more difficult or risky jumps if they deem them unnecessary to win against the rest of the field. (A *clean* performance is one with no noticeable mistakes—no falls, all jumps landed on one foot, spins fast and centered, footwork snappy and crisp.)

Because of the length of the long and the demands of its content, endurance and prior conditioning will play a part in a skater's performance. Most often, when skating the long a competitor will start strong, executing the more difficult maneuvers in order to grab the attention of the judges and audience. Toward the middle of the program, the music tempo will slow to allow the skater some recovery time—hopefully enough for the program to finish with a *bang!* Because of the length and the tremendous output of physical, mental, and emotional energy, sadly, some skaters simply fizzle out by the end of their long.

The long program counts as two thirds of a skater's overall score. It is judged much as the short is, with one mark for technical merit and one for presentation.

Skaters often perform more conservatively in the short, because even a small error can have significant consequences. In the long you'll see more of a tendency to go for it, with women often performing six or seven triple jumps and the men matching that, with an occasional quadruple or two attempted for good measure. Such expansiveness comes in part from the fact that a long-program mistake (usually a botched jump) can be overcome by a second attempt, hopefully with a successful outcome, later in the program. Still, even with the option of second attempts, numerous errors will reflect negatively in the overall scoring.

DISTINGUISHING JUMPS

When you're watching a live show or a TV broadcast with family and friends, their most frequently asked question is likely to be: "All the jumps look the same. How can you tell the difference?" Even if you've become proficient at executing your single Salchow, you may not be able to identify its big brother, the triple Salchow, when performed by a professional.

Let's take a look at the different aspects of the triple jumps in *descending* order of execution difficulty.

Triple Axel

The triple axel is fairly easy to distinguish, because it is the only multirevolution jump (besides the double and single axel) that launches from a *forward* outside edge. The skater takes off from the forward outside edge of one foot, rotates three and a half times in the air, and lands on the opposite foot, gliding on a backward outside edge.

Triple Lutz

The approach into the lutz is most often a prolonged *back* outside edge on the *left* foot (assuming the skater is right-handed). From that back outside edge glide, the skater will reach back with the *right* leg, plant the toe pick, vault into the air, rotate three times in a counterclockwise direction, and land backward on the right outside edge.

The difficulty in this jump stems from the fact that the entry edge should be curving away from the direction that the jump will travel. Even many top-ranked skaters have trouble maintaining this outside edge. As we mentioned earlier in the text, TV commentators often refer to an incorrect lutz takeoff as a "flutz"—because when improperly performed, the triple lutz becomes a triple *flip*.

Usually the setup for a triple lutz involves the skater gliding backward into one of the four corners of the rink. There's no special reason or magic to this approach. In a practice session, however, this is the desired setup, because it decreases the odds of collision with other skaters.

Triple Flip

It's very easy to confuse the triple flip with the triple lutz: The only technical difference is that entry edge. On the lutz the skater glides in on the back *outside* edge; with the flip it's the back *inside* edge. All other technical aspects of the jump remain the same.

To help you distinguish between the two, look for a skater to perform a left forward outside three turn going *into* the triple flip in order to achieve that back *inside* takeoff edge. (For the triple lutz, keep your eyes open for the *longer* back outside edge glide approach.) The three turn will be followed by a reach-back with the right leg and a vault off the right toe pick. The skater revolves three times in the air (counterclockwise) and lands on the right back *outside* edge.

Triple Loop

This is the *only* triple that takes off from and lands on the same foot. Most often, the entrance into the triple loop involves a curved, backward two-foot glide traveling counterclockwise. Look for the left foot to be slightly in front of the right, with the left arm in front and the right in back. It will appear to you as though the skater is jumping off *both* feet, although in reality the left foot leaves the ice first; the jump launches from the right back outside edge, revolves thrice, and lands, once again, on the right back outside edge.

Aside from being performed in isolation, the double or triple loop is one of two jumps (the other being the double or triple toe loop) that comprises the second jump in any jump combination.

Triple Salchow

Watch for the approach into the triple Salchow to come most often from a left forward outside three turn, although you may also see the jump performed from a right inside mohawk. In either case the skater will launch into the air from the left back inside edge of the turning foot. After the turn, the skater should be gliding backward in a counterclockwise curve. At the point of takeoff the back edge deepens slightly and the skater springs up off the left foot, rotates three times in the air, and lands backward on a right outside edge.

Observe very closely for the deepening of that takeoff edge—it's fairly subtle and happens quickly.

Triple Toe Loop

The triple toe loop can come from either of two entrances, both designed to give the skater a right back outside edge when entering the jump.

The first strategy involves the skater gliding forward into the jump. He then steps onto his right foot and performs a forward inside three turn, placing him onto a right back outside edge.

The second technique involves the skater executing a left forward outside three turn and then changing feet.

In either case, because this is a toe jump, the three turn will travel in a relatively straight line.

Once the skater is gliding backward on the right back outside edge, he will reach back with his left leg, plant his left toe pick into the ice, vault off it, and rotate three times in the air (counterclockwise) before landing on a right back outside edge. Be forewarned that it's very easy to confuse the triple toe with the triple flip and the triple lutz. However, the majority of skaters take off for the triple flip and the triple lutz from the *right* toe pick. On the triple toe loop they use the *left* toe pick.

Finally, remember that all triple jumps (and spins as well) revolve (or rotate) in the same direction—counterclockwise for righties, clockwise for lefties.

Jump Combinations

As we stated earlier, a jump combination is *required* for the short program and *recommended* for the long. The required jump combination consists of a triple jump *immediately* followed (with no additional steps or turns in between) by a second double or triple jump.

Watching skaters perform jump combinations on TV or at a live show can be deceptive—they make it look so easy! The reality of the triple-triple combination is that the technique on the first jump needs to be virtually *flawless* in order for the skater to have sufficient momentum and correct position to successfully complete the second jump.

When watching jump combinations, look for the second jump to be a double or a triple loop (where the skater has landed the first jump with the free leg in front, and then immediately jumps from the landing leg), or a double or triple *toe* loop (where the skater has landed the first jump with the left leg extended behind, proceeds to plant the left toe pick, and then vaults off it into the air).

IDENTIFYING SPINS

Identifying spins is much easier than differentiating between jumps. Let's take a look at some of the spins you'd see at a live or telecast event, keeping in mind that skaters can build unique variations from the core of the spin.

Scratch Spin and Back Scratch Spin

These are relatively simple spins to identify, because they are the only ones in which the skater is completely perpendicular to the ice. The spin usually begins slowly and builds momentum as the skater cuts resistance by pulling her arms and free leg in closer to the body. The regular scratch spin rotates counterclockwise and is most often executed on a left back inside edge. The back scratch spin also revolves counterclockwise but is performed on the back outside edge of the right foot.

Sit Spin

Given the name of this spin, it's not hard to guess what you'll be looking for. The skater spins in what appears to be a sitting position, with one leg extended to the front. Again, the sit spin revolves counterclockwise on a left back inside edge. Also look for the back sit (frequently done in combination with other positions), which rotates counterclockwise on the right back outside edge.

Camel Spin

Take your forward spiral (arabesque!), perform it while revolving counterclockwise on a left back inside edge, and you have a camel spin. We're not really sure where the name came from; unless your skating dress or shirt is bunched into a hump on your back, you don't really look like a camel. In any event, it is an impressive maneuver. As with the scratch and sit spins, there is also a back camel, which is performed on the right back outside edge.

Layback

A beautiful element, you'll see this spin performed primarily by ladies, although men are beginning to experiment with the layback as well. It has a number of variations.

It essentially begins as a one-foot spin, with the skater then pressing the hips and pelvis forward, arching the back, and dropping the head to the back or side. Free-leg and arm positions will vary greatly, and are limited only by the skater's creativity.

Flying Spins

These spins are initiated by some sort of jump or leap into the air. The two most common are the flying sit and the flying camel.

- **Flying Sit:** Look for a left forward outside entry edge into the flying sit spin. The skater will then leap straight up into the air from the left toe pick, tucking that left leg underneath, and extending the right leg slightly out to the side. Arms will be extended out to the side or slightly above shoulder height. The skater lands on the left back inside edge and immediately tucks into a sit-spin position.
- **Flying Camel:** The skater enters the jump from a sharp left forward outside edge. It will appear as if the right leg is

thrown strongly up and out to the side as the skater springs off the left toe and snaps the left leg out and back. The skater lands on the right foot, spinning in the back-camel position.

Spin Combinations

Any of the above-mentioned spins can be grouped together to form what is called a combination spin. These spins can involve both a change of foot and a change of position with no interruption in the flow of the spin.

One example of a combination spin is camel to back camel to back sit. Another is camel to layback to back sit.

WHY WATCH

We believe there are many benefits to viewing figure skating as a spectator, whether you're watching a live or a televised event. Here are a few of them:

- You can practice your new jump and spin identification skills, along with deepening your understanding of the scoring system.
- Watching the technique, elements, and choreography of top skaters may assist you in designing routines for yourself.
- Attending a live show may afford you the opportunity to meet top amateur and professional skaters. If this happens, have the courage to ask these individuals skating-related questions: "How long did it take you to master your axel? Did you always have the same coach or have you had several over the years? What spin or jump has given you the most trouble? How do you control your jitters before a big competition?"
- If you're experiencing a flat spot in your own skating, watching any type of event can help inspire or reignite a passion for your sport.

In the short program there are limitations as to the number of foot changes and number of positions. There's also a required number of revolutions on each foot.

In the long program, however, once again, anything goes. Skaters are free to exercise their creativity and spinning ability, performing any number of position changes in one particular spin.

EXHIBITION SKATING

In exhibition events away from the judges' critical eyes, skaters perform routines designed strictly for entertainment purposes. There are absolutely no limitations on content, and you'll see skaters loosen up under the noncompetitive conditions. In these displays of figure skating talent, the only judging per se comes from the audience showing its approval with enthusiastic applause. Here's where you'll see the individual personalities of the skaters emerge and shine. Some experiment with avant-garde or "against-type" routines and programs as they explore different aspects of artistic expression.

HOLIDAY SHOWS, TRAVELING TROUPES, THEME SHOWS, MADE-FOR-TV EVENTS

At Christmastime various production companies will put together holiday figure skating shows that feature songs and characters in tune with the season—skating Santas and snowmen and the like. Some of these productions will take to the road, visiting various cities and featuring name skaters and/or relative unknowns. Other holiday shows are produced exclusively for TV.

Traveling troupes come in all shapes and sizes, and usually feature casts of well-known skaters who perform a variety of numbers. This type of show would fall into the category of exhibition skating.

Theme shows usually center on a well-known fable, fairy tale, or feature film (usually animated) that has done well at the box office.

This past year we caught a version of *The Wizard of Oz* on ice. The show was superb, and although the skaters were relative unknowns, their skating and acting skills were top shelf. Individually, the principals (the main characters) pulled off some impressive double and triple jumps, dazzling spins, and elegant connecting moves, all in the context of telling the story. The group numbers—where cast members (not the principals) skated in unison much as in synchronized team skating—were equally convincing.

Theme shows can also be produced solely for TV. The ones we've seen in the past few years usually have at least one or two World or Olympic champions as the lead draws.

Lastly, the past several years have seen a spate of "competitions" put together by network or cable TV. Often these events feature celebrity judges, and the standards for scoring certainly don't match what you'd see at the National, World, and Olympic levels. It's best to look at these events primarily in the category of entertainment.

Finally, we're going to let you in on a little secret.

Ever notice that in most of the holiday, theme, or exhibition skating shown on TV, the performers never seem to fall? Jumps are always landed, spins always stay centered, nobody ever slips or loses an edge. Ever wonder why?

They edit out the goofs!

That's right; these shows are *taped.* If a skater falls or bails out of a jump, the producers can leave the mistakes on the cutting room floor.

We discovered this little trick several years ago when we attended a live exhibition show that was also being taped for telecast at a later date. During the course of the live show, we saw skaters pop jumps, fall on landings, and blow spins. Since the overall show was top notch and because imperfections are a *reality* in skating, we forgave the flaws.

At the conclusion of the show, after the thunderous applause had died down and the skaters had left the ice, we began to file out of our seats. It was then that one of the principals in the show—a great skater and one of the most engaging entertainers in the business—came back out onto the ice, microphone in hand.

"Where are you going?" he asked.

The crowd chuckled.

"Want to see some more skating?" he then teased.

A collective roar went up from the crowd.

He instructed us to go back to our seats and went on to explain that a TV audience is not as forgiving as a live crowd. The troupe was therefore going to *reshoot* most of the missed falls and other errors that had occurred during the show.

One by one, the skaters who had flubbed came back onto the ice and attempted the element until they got it right (sometimes only after repeated tries). The producers had obviously marked the mistakes so the music was timed to synchronize exactly with the execution of the element. The whole process took about 45 minutes.

Several weeks later we watched the telecast version of the show we had seen live.

It was flawless.

CHAPTER 15

WHERE TO NOW?

I soon realized that no journey carries one far unless, as it extends into the world around us, it goes an equal distance into the world within.

—Lillian Smith

SKATING AND THE FAMILY

Both the Schallehns and the Tashmans started skating as a family activity. It's quite common to see a mom, a dad, and a passel of kids all lacing up for a learn-to-skate program. Today only three members of both families—all females—still skate. The others, by design or default, have all left the sport.

Loss of interest, interest in other activities (sports, hobbies, dating), finances, and injury top the list as to why individuals will choose to exit the rink—forever.

Let's take a closer look at the *ways* and *whys* of when a skater says good-bye.

LOSS OF INTEREST

At times you may find that you have to practically drag yourself (or your skating kid) to the rink. The sessions are lifeless and lackluster;

merely the thought of lifting yourself into the air for a jump exhausts you. Deep inside you feel a smoldering frustration. Is it burnout? Depression? Lyme disease?

In all likelihood you've hit a plateau. And *all* skaters have "been there, done that." With a plateau you've simply hit the ceiling of your learning capabilities . . . for now. Your expectations of where you thought you'd be at this stage of your skating career don't equal what you're putting out in performance.

When you hit a plateau, accept where you are, because you will soon pass through it. Your body-mind learns at its own rate and pace. Fighting or getting angry about the situation only makes it worse.

Burnout is another story. Perhaps you've been spending too much time on your program, on a certain jump or spin, or at the rink in general. We just heard a collective gasp from all the diehards—but in all seriousness maybe you do need a little break.

Your break can come either on or off the ice. Take a day or two and try working on elements *other* than that elusive axel or the layback that just won't center. If your coach is cracking the whip a little too hard in preparation for an upcoming event, maybe it's time for a heart-to-heart talk with her about lightening the touch. Some coaches get more nervous than their students before a test session or a competition.

Writer Clarissa Pinkola Estes recommends that if your creativity becomes stale in one discipline, go observe others engaged in *different* creative ventures. Take a few days or a full week off from skating and go to the live theater or a performance of the ballet, listen to a live band, or watch that guy with the bulging biceps make a pepperoni pizza. In all probability you'll return to the rink refreshed and renewed.

Some parents and coaches push young skaters too hard. If your child appears to be reaching burnout, have that heart-to-heart with either her or, if necessary, her coach. Remember, this activity has to have a strong element of fun in order for it to stay a priority in a skater's life. Most kids and adults recover from burnout, but some don't. It's always heartbreaking to see a youngster leave the sport angry and broken from an overzealous parent or coach.

The last possibility is that you, or your skating child, have truly experienced a loss of interest in figure skating. Our friend Dave got it into his head a few years back that he wanted to be a sky diver. He went out and read every book available on the subject, watched videos, took ground school classes, and finally signed up for his first jump.

After that jump, we asked him about the experience. We were expecting to hear exclamations about the incredible rush, the ultimate natural high, the adrenaline flow, that sort of stuff. With an incredible flatness of expression, he answered, "It was okay."

Okay? Does this guy have a pulse? He's free-falling from the great blue yonder and all he can muster is a weak "okay"? Yes, that was, and remains, his reality.

The point here is that the *actual activity* didn't match his *fantasy* of what he believed skydiving would be. Travel posters can inspire magnificent "mind pictures" of far-off destinations. Arriving at your destination, however, the reality sometimes doesn't even come close. If you've sampled figure skating and found that it doesn't generate sufficient interest to keep you coming back to the rink . . . that's okay!

Life is a banquet, a treasure trove of new experiences, adventures, and challenges. Go out into the world, explore, sample, and discover what *will* seize and hold your passion.

INTEREST IN OTHER ACTIVITIES

With the onset of adolescence, teenage skaters may find themselves distracted—clothing, hairstyles, school clubs and organizations, celebrities, and the opposite sex can all grab attention. Belonging to a group and attaining in-school popularity often become paramount to the young adult.

When Peggy Sue announces to her papa that she's no longer going to skate on the weekends because it cuts into her social life, you know there'll soon be a storm raging in that household, especially because Papa just invested in $400 custom boots and $300 top-of-the-line blades for his ice princess.

Compound this with the fact that Peggy Sue just signed up for drama club on Tuesdays and Thursdays—the other two days of the week scheduled for skating—and her dresses and skates may be the top items at her club's upcoming next-to-new sale.

If you're the parent of a teen skater who has decided to leave skating for various other activities, our advice is to let her go. She may come back to the sport, she may not. But forcing an adolescent into committing to skating will usually result only in building resentment, if not outright hatred.

If you are the parent of a skater, the chauffeur to the rink, and the main financier, you need to realize that figure skating is not orthodontia.

Here's what we mean: With orthodontia you always get a predictable outcome—straight teeth. The investment of time and money into figure skating *never* has a predictable outcome.

Like we said, allow your teenager to walk away from the sport with dignity and her head held high, and she may come back to it . . . in her twenties, thirties, or middle age. She may find a renewed interest when her *own* children express a desire to take to the ice. And what better gift could she pass on to her own kids than the skills she herself learned as a youngster?

If you're an adult skater, other sports and hobbies may draw you away. During the summer you may want to spend whatever precious free time you have on a golf course or a tennis court, not the confines of a rink. Again, an interest in figure skating may run in cycles. Waking up to a brisk winter morning may inspire you to dust off your blades and head out to your favorite pond for an hour of simple stroking.

Always remember: This sport is about enjoyment. If that slips away, move on.

FINANCES

Here's a financial rule of thumb: Your skating bills will increase in direct proportion to the amount of time and energy you invest in your sport.

Earlier in the book we defined a *recreational* skater as one who skates one to three times per week. But let's suppose that you want to be a high-level competitor, with aspirations of someday skating in Olympic or World competition or with a traveling troupe of skaters in the tradition of Ice Capades or Disney on Ice.

Without posting actual dollar amounts—which vary geographically—let's look at just a few of the places where you'll need to spend money:

- **Ice fees:** Three to seven days per week, sometimes several sessions per day

- **Coaching fees,** including all or part of her travel and lodging expenses during competitions
- **Equipment fees:** Boots and blades, replaced on an as-needed basis
- **Clothing fees:** Competition apparel, tights, practice dresses, skirts, shirts, and pants
- **Competition fees:** Entry fees, travel, food, lodging

It is an unfortunate fact of life that some families and solo skaters are squeezed out of figure skating due to financial constraints. It would be nice to believe that we could predict and completely ensure our financial futures, but that's just not the case. Dad or Mom loses a job, a brother or a sister needs money for college, an unexpected legal situation drains the family finances—and suddenly funding for figure skating has to be cut, if not eradicated altogether.

ACCIDENTS AND INJURIES

They happen. Even with your protective gear, you can't control fate.

As figure skaters progress to higher levels, their helmets are soon discarded. Some females wear high ponytails in an attempt to cushion the blow of backward falls. (And you thought all those pretty misses were just making a fashion statement!) Compression shorts—those cycling shorts with padding sewn into the tailbone and hip areas—are also retired. As some girls reach adolescence, they grow concerned that the shorts may make them look too "hippy." Thick sponges, the kind used to wash cars, are then stuffed into the clothing covering the hip and tailbone areas. We gather that, although the lump is much larger than what's seen with compression shorts, there is no confusion as to where the body ends and the sponge starts.

Still, even with safety equipment and a mind-set of skating defensively, injuries that end a skater's career do happen.

If an injury occurs that requires medical attention, your personal physician and/or a specialist (if needed) will be the ones to suggest or mandate the action to be taken.

It may be an injury that will heal, and you'll be back on the ice in no time flat. Perhaps the injury may require surgery and a period of convalescence before you return to the rink. Or the injury, with or without surgery, may be such that your physician recommends you discontinue skating—permanently.

Injuries can happen on or off the ice. They can occur while participating in another sport, while riding in a car or on a motorcycle or bike, or when walking down the street.

Really. Bernie was walking down the street minding his own business when the cartilage in his right knee decided to tear. After surgery, his physician told him that running and speed skating needed to be dropped from his leisuretime repertoire. His bicycling could remain.

If an injury happens, and your physician mandates or recommends deleting figure skating from your physical activities, feel free to get second and third opinions. But keep in mind that fate, age, and reality sometimes force the end of your active relationship with skating.

If that were to happen, consider that the world of figure skating may still hold a place for you—as a judge, a coach, a volunteer in your club, an ardent fan at both amateur and professional competitions and exhibitions.

BUT WHAT IF . . .

Your finances hold steady, you remain injury-free, and the light of your passion for figure skating glows brighter with each passing day. And with it, your aspirations for the future hold the dream of someday skating at high amateur or professional levels.

One question you may ask is, "Do I really have the talent?"

We've always been curious about exactly what constitutes talent, so over the years we've put that question to many people. Here are some of the answers we've received:

- Perseverance and dedication
- The "it" quality (that undefinable trait many skating pros claim they see when they see talent)
- Luck and lucky breaks
- Fate
- The ability to pass skating tests quickly
- Balance, athleticism, and a certain aggressiveness

As you can see, we found no consensus of opinion. So our suggestion to you is a simple one.

Follow your heart.

For us, skating has always been a metaphor for life itself. One moment you're experiencing all the glory of gliding gracefully along, the next moment you fall flat on your rear end. And then to pick yourself up, dust yourself off, and begin anew!

You may be on that bus for the next Winter Games, having won a berth on the Olympic team. Should it be you, let us be the first to wish you the best of luck and good fortune. But always remember, whether it be in an Olympic arena or on your backyard pond, in our eyes you're a champion each and every time you step onto the ice.

Happy skating!

GLOSSARY

Arabesque—an artistic maneuver where the skater glides on one leg while bent forward at the waist, with the other leg fully extended behind. Arabesques can be performed forward or backward on either edge. Also referred to as a *spiral*.

Axel—the first multirevolution jump taught. Easily recognized, because it is the only multirevolution jump that launches from a forward edge. An axel takes off from a forward outside edge, rotates one and a half revolutions in the air, and lands on the other foot, gliding on a back outside edge.

Barrier (Boards)—the wall surrounding the actual ice surface at an indoor and some outdoor rinks. Also known as *dasher boards*.

Blade guards (or skate guards)—hard rubber or plastic scabbards or sheaths used to protect the blades when walking in skates on any surface other than ice.

Blades—the chrome-plated steel runners mounted on the bottom of the skating boot.

Boot—the part of the skate that actually encases the foot and the ankle. Quality boots are made of leather and tightened with a combination of laces and eyelets.

Bunny hop—a beginning jump that launches from a forward glide. The skater vaults off one foot, kicks the other leg forward, touches down on the toe pick of the kicking leg, and lands gliding forward on the starting foot.

Camel spin—a spin on one foot in which the lower chest and stomach are parallel to the ice and the free leg is extended high behind the body and horizontal to the ice. Also known as a *parallel spin*.

Carriage—a term frequently used when describing a skater's posture.

Center—the meeting place for the long and short axes in a compulsory figure, as well as in the waltz eight on the Pre-Preliminary Moves in the Field test.

Centering—the ability to stay in one spot on the ice when performing a spin.

Change of edge—a movement in which the skater goes from one edge to the other without changing feet. Involves a weight shift by the upper body.

Check—a movement performed at the completion of a jump or spin that enables the skater to stop rotating. The term is also used to describe the cross pressure and releasing shoulder action used to execute a three turn or mohawk.

Chief referee—the head honcho in charge of a test session or competition.

Choreography—a routine of jumps, spins, footwork, and connecting moves developed to interpret a specific piece of music.

Combination jump—a series of at least two jumps performed in sequence with no steps or turns in between.

Combination spin—a spin combining two or more changes in position and one or more changes of feet.

Competing against the book—when a skater is the sole competitor in an event, she or he competes against a perfect score. Seen only in ISI competitions.

Compulsory dance—one of more than 30 dances developed for testing and competition. Compulsory dances have a prescribed pattern that traverses the ice surface. They also have specific steps, and each dance has its own distinctive rhythm and tempo.

Compulsory figures—a series of exercises designed to be performed in a variety of figure-eight patterns. Includes many different types of turns, edge changes, and loops. Designed to promote upper- and lower-body control, strength, edge quality, correct blade usage, and good posture.

Crossover—a specific type of skating stroke, performed either forward or backward, in which one foot pushes and then crosses in front of the other. Crossovers are used primarily to generate speed.

Double jump—a jump that lifts off, rotates two full turns in the air, and then lands gliding backward on an outside edge (with the exception of a double axel, which rotates two and a half times around).

Edge—the inner or outer side of the blade that is actually in contact with the ice when the skater is moving on a curve.

Edge jump—a jump that launches directly from the edge of the blade on which the skater is gliding, without assistance from the toe pick.

Flat—when the skater is gliding in a straight line with both sides of the blade in contact with the ice ("gliding on a flat").

Flight—the group of skaters against whom you compete.

Flip jump—a jump that launches from the back inside edge of one foot and the toe pick of the other foot, rotates 360 degrees, and then lands on the back outside edge of the picking foot.

Flooding—the act of spraying water across a flat surface to create a smooth, uniform sheet of ice.

Flow—to glide along smoothly and swiftly without noticeable effort.

Flying camel spin—a spin initiated by a jump from which the skater lands spinning in a back camel position.

Flying sit spin—a spin where the skater leaps into the air with one leg tucked underneath and the other leg extended out to the side; the skater then lands on the leg that was tucked under and immediately assumes the sit-spin position.

Free dance—a choreographed routine performed by a dance team. The routine is comprised primarily of intricate footwork sequences and dance steps and is skated to music with strong dance tempos.

Free side—the side of the body above the foot that is off the ice.

Freestyle—the discipline in figure skating that incorporates jumps and spins.

Glide—to move smoothly across the ice, on either one foot or two.

Hockey stop—a stopping action best recognized for the spray of ice shavings it produces.

Hollow—the curved area between the outside and inside edges on the bottom of the blade.

Ice Skating Institute (ISI)—one of figure skating's three governing bodies. The ISI often bills itself as catering to the "recreational" ice skater.

Inside edge—the edge of the skate blade closest to the inside of the leg.

International Skating Union (ISU)—the international governing body of amateur skating.

Invitational competition—a USFSA competition open to all skaters who are members in good standing of a USFSA club.

Kilian position—a dance hold with partners located hip to hip; the woman is to the man's right.

Layback spin—a one-foot spin where the skater presses her hips and pelvis forward, arches her back, and drops her head either to the back or to the side. Free-leg and arm positions vary.

Lobe—in ice dancing, a term that refers to a step or series of steps that travel on the same curve, creating a semicircle on the ice. In compulsory figures the term refers to a full circle.

Long axis—an imaginary line through the middle of the rink (or of a figure eight) that divides it lengthwise into two equal sides.

Long program—terminology used in competitive skating to describe the freestyle routine, whose content is unlimited.

Loop—a smaller compulsory figure (its diameter is the skater's height) in which a teardrop-shaped loop is formed within the larger circle.

Loop jump—a jump that launches off the back outside edge of one skate, rotates one full turn in the air, and lands gliding backward on the outside edge of the same skate.

Lunge—an accent move in which the skater bends deeply into one knee while the other leg extends behind, blade off the ice, side of boot skimming the ice surface.

Lutz jump—a jump that launches from the back outside edge of one foot and the toe pick of the other foot, rotates 360 degrees, and lands on the back outside edge of the picking foot.

Mohawk—a turn from forward to backward or backward to forward in which the skater changes feet as the turn occurs. It starts on one edge and turns onto the same edge.

Mounting—affixing a blade to the bottom of the skating boot.

Moves in the Field—a series of exercises devised to replace compulsory figures.

Outside edge—the edge of the blade closest to the outside of the leg.

Patch—a rectangle of ice where individual skaters practice their compulsory figures.

Pivot—a maneuver in which the toe pick of one skate is planted and remains in the ice while the other skate circles around it.

Pop—a term used to describe a skater going up for a jump and then bailing out, usually by checking her arms out mid-air, or never assuming an air position conducive to rotation.

Presentation mark—one of the two sets of marks awarded in competitive figure skating; also called the artistic mark. Refers to choreography, musical interpretation, posture, extension, and overall appeal.

Print—the tracing left on the ice by the skate blade.

Program—the term for the skater's routine that is choreographed to music.

Progressive—a series of steps performed on the same lobe; frequently used to describe a step sequence in a compulsory dance.

Pumping—a means of gaining momentum while skating forward or backward on two feet.

Push-off—the act of thrusting off one foot and gliding on the other.

Quad (quadruple jump)—a jump with four full rotations in the air, with the exception of the quad axel, which is four and a half rotations.

Radius—the curve between the outside and inside edges on the bottom of the blade.

Regional competition—the first qualifying competition a skater must participate in to become eligible for the U.S. National Championship. The skaters who place first, second, third, and, occasionally, fourth at a regional competition then qualify to compete at the sectional level.

Required elements—1) the specific skills a skater must demonstrate mastery of in order to pass a test. 2) the designated skills (jumps, spins, step sequences) that comprise a short program.

Reskate—when, in a testing situation, a judge or referee requests that the skater repeat the execution of a required element.

Retry—when skaters don't meet the minimum passing standard for a USFSA test, they are given the option to "retry" the test.

Salchow—a jump off the back inside edge of one foot that rotates one turn in the air and lands on the other foot gliding on a back outside edge.

School figures—an older term for compulsory figures.

Scratch spin—an upright spin on one foot. It's also referred to as an *upright spin, one-foot spin,* or *blur spin.*

Scribe—a compasslike instrument used to draw circles on the ice when practicing compulsory figures.

Serpentine—a three-lobed compulsory figure; also used to describe a pattern of footwork that covers three different lobes on the ice.

Short axis—an imaginary line through the middle of a figure that goes through the center and is perpendicular to the long axis.

Short program—a competitive routine whose content is limited to specific elements designated by the USFSA or the ISU. Also known as the *technical program.*

Single jump—a jump that lifts off, rotates 360 degrees in the air, and comes down backward (with the exception of the single axel, which revolves one and a half times in the air before landing).

Sit spin—a spin in which the skater rotates in a sitting position with one leg extended to the front.

Skating dads—see *Skating moms.* Same attributes, different sex.

Skating moms—at their best, loving mothers who provide physical, financial, and emotional support for their skating child; at their worst, parents who obsessively push and prod a skating child, primarily seeking a vicarious pleasure should the youngster do well in the competitive aspect of the sport. Very similar to stage mothers and Little League dads.

Snowplow stop—a braking method, usually for beginners, where the skates are parallel to each other and then push out to the sides to create a stop.

Stroke—the pushing and gliding movement performed by a skater to gain momentum.

Swizzle—a beginner's technique for gaining backward or forward momentum.

Synchronized team skating—a discipline of figure skating in which skaters perform as a team, creating different formations on the ice in unison. Formerly known as precision team skating.

Technical merit—a mark awarded to the skater reflecting the difficulty and correctness of the performed elements.

Technical program—see *Short program*.

Three turn—a one-foot turn from forward to backward or backward to forward in which the skater changes edge in the middle of the turn. The name of the turn is derived from the tracing that the blade leaves on the ice, which is shaped like the numeral 3.

Toe jump—a type of jump that launches with an assist from the toe pick of one skate.

Toe loop—a jump that launches from the toe pick of one skate, rotates 360 degrees, and lands on the back outside edge of the other skate blade.

Toe pick—the serrated teeth located on the front of the blade.

Toe push—an incorrect method of pushing in which the skater uses only the toe pick rather than the entire length of the blade.

Tracing—the mark left behind by the blade as it travels across the ice.

Traveling—when, during a spin, the skater incorrectly traverses across the ice rather than centering the spin.

Triple jump—a jump that lifts off, rotates three times in the air, and lands backward (with the exception of the triple axel, which rotates three and a half times).

T-stop—a braking maneuver in which the skater is gliding forward on one foot, then places the other foot down behind the skating foot and perpendicular to it.

United States Figure Skating Association (USFSA)—one of figure skating's two governing bodies in the United States.

Waltz jump—a half-turn jump that launches from the forward outside edge of one skate and lands on the back outside edge of the other skate. It is usually the first rotation jump taught to beginning free skaters.

Zamboni—The vehicle, powered either by propane or batteries, used to smooth and resurface the ice.

RELATED
FIGURE-SKATING WORDS,
TERMS, AND PHRASES

Artificial ice or "plastic ice"—a skatable surface used when lack of refrigeration or climate does not permit water to freeze.

Bracket—a means of turning from forward to backward or backward to forward in which the skater changes edge at the top of the turn. The point of the bracket turn always faces out of the lobe.

Canadian Figure Skating Association (CFSA)—the governing body of amateur figure skating in Canada.

Centered spin—a technically correct spin in which the skater remains in the same spot on the ice while spinning.

Chassé—an ice dance maneuver in which the skater strokes onto one foot, pulls the feet together, and then slightly lifts the original skating foot, keeping its blade relatively parallel to the ice.

Cheated jump—a technically incorrect jump in which part of the rotation is done on the ice (on either the takeoff or landing) instead of in the air.

Choctaw—a two-foot turn similar to the mohawk where the skater turns from forward to backward or backward to forward. While a mohawk turns from one edge to the same edge, a choctaw turns from one edge to a different edge. There are numerous variations to the choctaw—forward outside to back inside, back outside to forward inside, and more. The choctaw is most frequently used in ice dance, Moves in the Field, and footwork sequences.

Counter—a type of turn that travels from one edge to the same edge while changing lobes, with the cusp (point) of the turn facing into the new lobe.

Ina Bauer—an accent or artistic move similar to the spread eagle but with the front leg bent and the back leg straight. See *Spread eagle*.

Losing your jumps—a phenomenon in which a skater loses the ability to execute a previously mastered jump. This loss can be brief (one or two days) or long term. Theories vary, but most attribute the loss of a jump to a loss of confidence.

Olympia—the brand name of a vehicle designed to clean and resurface the ice. It was developed after the patent for the Zamboni expired.

Rocker—a turn from forward to backward or backward to forward in which the skater begins to turn as if executing a three turn, but then remains on the same edge and changes lobes. The turn will point into the original lobe.

Scratching—when a skater chooses not to test or compete, for a variety of reasons, after previously registering to do so.

Skating a clean program—performing all the elements in your routine without noticeable errors.

Skating down—when a skater tends to not perform as well in competition as in practice. Usually attributed to excessive nerves or stage fright.

Skating up—1) in invitational USFSA competitions only, when a skater chooses to compete at a higher level than his or her documented test status. 2) when a skater rises to the occasion—skating better in performance than during practice sessions. The opposite of *skating down*.

Spread eagle—an interpretive move in which the skater is gliding on both skates that are placed on the same edge. The heels of the skates point toward each other and the toes point away.

INDEX

Page references in *italics* refer to illustrations.